"*Tim Leffel's* Make Your Travel Dollars Worth a Fortune *is full of solid advice and undeniable principles of smart travel.*"

— Arthur Frommer

MAKE YOUR TRAVEL DOLLARS WORTH A FORTUNE

The Contrarian Traveler's Guide to Getting More for Less

Tim Leffel

Travelers' Tales
Palo Alto

Travelers' Tales and Travelers' Tales Guides are trademarks of
Travelers' Tales, Inc. 853 Alma Street, Palo Alto, California 94301.

Art Direction: Stefan Gutermuth
Interior Design: Kathryn Heflin and Susan Bailey
Cover Illustration: © Tahiti Tourisme
Page layout: Cynthia Lamb

Distributed by: Publishers Group West, 1700 Fourth Street,
Berkeley, California 94710.

Library of Congress Cataloging-in-Publication Data

Leffel, Tim.
   Make your travel dollars worth a fortune : the contrarian traveler's
guide to getting more for less / by Tim Leffel. — 1st ed.
      p. cm.
   Includes bibliographical references and index.
   ISBN-13: 978-1-932361-39-1 (pbk. : alk. paper)
   ISBN-10: 1-932361-39-1 (alk. paper)
1. Travel. I. Title.
   G151.L45 2006
   910.4—dc22
                         2006017688

First Edition
Printed in the United States
10 9 8 7 6 5 4 3 2 1

To Donna
For dragging me off the work
treadmill and then being by my
side on five continents.

Table of Contents

Introduction

How Do You Make Your Travel Dollars Worth a Fortune?

"I will go to my grave claiming that the less you spend, the more you enjoy, the more authentic the experience it is, the more profound, the more exciting, the more unexpected."

—Arthur Frommer, interviewed in A *Sense of Place*

A cartoon shows a couple exiting the airplane, suitcases in hand. The woman says, "That was the trip of a lifetime!" The man says, "Good thing, because that's how long we'll be paying for it."

For far too many travelers, this isn't a joke.

This book is a tale about two kinds of travelers: those who pay more than they need to by doing it the standard way, and those who make their travel dollars worth a fortune by choosing a different path. Those who travel like sheep and those who don't.

Living somewhere in Anytown, USA is a very average American couple named Mr. and Mrs. Smith. Last year they took a very typical vacation. They talked about where they wanted to go and decided that London would be nice. They couldn't put their finger on why, but they agreed that they had always wanted to go there. "Summer seems to be the time to go," they agreed, "probably because the weather is nice then."

They checked into vacation packages soon after. "I didn't realize it was so expensive to go to London," said Mr. Smith. Neither had been reading the financial news and had no idea the dollar had declined 25% against the pound. They did not do any research about seasons, so they had no idea that summer is the most expensive time to fly.

After some cursory checking around, the Smiths booked a package containing a flight, six nights in a chain hotel whose name they recognized, and a rental car for three days. They were flying that airline for the first time and it wasn't connected to any of their frequent-flyer plans. They weren't quite sure where the hotel was, but the description said "central London." Since they had a rental car for three days, they immediately set about making plans for day trips to Bath, Cambridge, and Brighton. "Might as well get our money's worth," said Mrs. Smith. Online they bought theater tickets for two nights and they made a detailed list of every museum and site they wanted to see.

The flight didn't earn the Smiths any useful mileage and since it wasn't connected to any program where they did have a lot of mileage, they could not upgrade their ticket. They sat in a cramped coach cabin for seven hours. The hotel room was tiny, routine, and far from any subway station. They spent hundreds of dollars on taxis and could not walk to anywhere for dinner in the evenings. The restaurants they did go to, mostly ones featured in their guidebook or the magazine in their hotel room, were forgettable. They found out they could have bought theater tickets to the shows they attended for half-price if they had waited until the day of the show. They were exhausted from their long day trips out of town and ended up scratching the car twice because they weren't used to driving on the left side of the road. They ended up missing some of the London attractions on their list for lack of time, despite spending six or eight hours a day sightseeing. "Who knew the British Museum was so big?" Mrs. Smith asked.

The flight home was grueling and all the expensive souvenirs they bought made the trek through airports and customs even more difficult than it had been on the first leg. In the end, the Smiths spent a fortune on their vacation, but didn't really enjoy it that much. Both badly needed to get some extra sleep for the following week and were dragging at work. They winced when they opened their hefty credit card bill.

Does any of this story sound familiar? Not to the Johnsons. They spend half as much and enjoy their trips twice as much. Come along and see how they do it.

GETTING AWAY FROM THE HERDS

This book is subtitled "The Contrarian Traveler's Guide to Getting More for Less," because it takes some alternative action to really make your travel dollars worth more. You could describe the "contrarian traveler" with many words: uncommon, adaptive, astute, resourceful, or savvy. The idea is that by taking the left fork in the road, while everyone else is taking the right fork, these people are able to save a bundle, and get a better experience for their money, every time they travel. If you yin while everyone else yangs, you're almost guaranteed to get a better deal.

A study by the National Academy of Sciences found that mice and humans react the same way when trying to escape a crowded room. The scientists set up a model based on where the exits were and it worked every time—mice and men both defy logic and rush together with a like mind. Another study conducted at Emory University found that chimps are conformists. When one chimp was taught how to retrieve food, he or she would teach that method to the group. Even if other chimps were trained individually on different methods later, they soon abandoned them for the more popular group technique.

Fortunately, when we take time to think, we can do better than mice or monkeys. A report on the September 11 terrorist attacks, written by the National Institute on Standards and Technology, found that at least 2,500 World Trade Center lives were saved because people ignored what authorities told them to do. They heard the official advice to stay put, decided it was stupid, and got the hell out of there.

Going against the tide does require a bit of sense and a willingness to think independently. Being "contrarian" is a common theme in the financial world when it comes to investment decisions. The typical individual investor sells low and buys high, time and time again. An academic study that looked at the actions of U.S. mutual fund investors over time classified them as "short-term-return chasers" who move as "lemminglike masses." To get rich, the authors surmised, all you have to do is watch what the masses are doing and take a different path. Buy when there's a panic, sell when there's euphoria. The contrarian investor wins. Sounds easy, but most people can't stick with it.

There is a similar lemminglike movement in travel. Nearly everything you read touts the same predictable, expensive path. There are good reasons for this, which I'll go over in the first chapter, but the bottom line is that you are not likely to read a lot of advice about getting a truly good, "against the grain" travel deal in your local newspaper or glossy travel magazine. (There are exceptions, which I'll point you to later.) What I will provide in this book is a base of solid principles you can use to get better values each and every time you travel.

This is a guide to saving money on travel by avoiding "the peaks": peak crowds, peak seasons, peak destinations, and peak hotels, to name a few. This book will show you how to get the best deals every time by looking at each angle, not just at the most obvious costs, such as airfare. By following the easy-to-remember strategies outlined here, you will find ways not only to save money this year, but to save money each vacation for the rest of your life.

Here is a rundown on what you can expect to get out of *Make Your Travel Dollars Worth a Fortune.*

1. You will learn simple, easy-to-remember principles that will save you a huge amount of cash every time you travel.

2. You will learn why most people pay more than they need to for travel and find out how to avoid the traps that can drain your wallet.

3. You will learn how to see the big picture and determine which portion of your expenses can have the biggest payoff in terms of savings.

4. You will learn how to prioritize your requirements or desires to figure out which items are priorities and which ones are open to more flexible options.

5. When you are finished with this book, you should be able to make up for the cover price a hundred times over if you continue to follow just one chapter's worth of tips.

TWO COUPLES AND MANY PATHS...

Two imaginary couples will provide ongoing examples throughout this book. I've randomly called them the Smiths and the Johnsons. The Smiths will be very typical travelers: they shop for travel in the manner that most vacationers do, go to the destinations most other travelers go, and spend money at that location in the same ways that typical vacationers there do. As a result, they commonly spend up to a month's worth of take-home wages while away and are usually unable to afford more than one vacation per year.

The Johnsons, on the other hand, will be our contrarian travelers. They routinely use many of the techniques outlined in this book, generally doing the opposite of what the travel herds around them are doing. They think through the options and do their homework before they act. As a result, they spend a fraction of what the typical couple has spent and are able to travel better or more often as a result.

If your last name happens to be Smith or Johnson, don't take it personally either way. These names were chosen to embody the everyman and everywoman whose research and choices determine how much they pay. Nobody of any name, race, heritage, hometown, or education level has an advantage over another when making money-saving and trip-enhancing travel decisions. (Unless you're a citizen of Cuba or North Korea and can't leave the country, of course!) The advice in this book is for any reader who will take the time to do a little research and make good decisions, whether you are going to a destination one town over from your own or going completely around the world over the course of a year.

Throughout this book, we will look at the basic decisions any traveler makes before and during a trip. We'll examine the variables that factor into all aspects of travel. We'll ask the key questions, such as, "Is there a more economical way to do this that will still provide the experience we want?" or "Could we find a better bang for our buck somewhere else?"

While a bit of the guidance contained in this book will be relevant to long-term travelers and backpackers, this is by no means a shoestring travel guide. In my younger days I stayed in more cheap guesthouses than I would like to count. I have ridden buses where one person was holding a live chicken, another man was selling grilled rats on a stick, and there was a live pig squealing on the roof. I have also been waited on hand and foot in some of the most opulent hotels in the world. I have traveled single and as half of a romantic couple, plus I have experienced the unique challenges of traveling with a small child—both within the U.S. and internationally. This book will cover all the bases. The principles here are aimed at anyone who wants a better value for their travel budget, whether that budget is tiny or lavish. The common denominator is attitude. This is meant to be a how-to guide for getting a great deal, whether your journey is for one weekend or one year, in bamboo bungalows or surrounded by marble.

I've traveled a lot, but there are plenty of people who know more than I do about some subjects. So you'll also read lots of advice from experts with their own spin on specific aspects of travel, on subjects such as home exchanges, the value of loyalty, dining, and living abroad.

WHAT WILL YOU DO WITH THE SAVINGS?

If you could save $500 to $1,000 next time you went on vacation, what would you do with that extra money? Would you travel a few days longer? Or would you upgrade your experience and spend the money on better rooms, or on first-class train rides? I couldn't care less—I just want to make sure you are getting the most out of your budget. Decide what you value most and make that your priority. If you are able to explore the rainforest for ten days instead of five, great! If you're able to eat and drink to your heart's content on that long weekend instead of scrutinizing the menu prices, that's great, too! If you just want to take a long enough vacation to truly unwind and get through some of those books and magazines you've been meaning to read, terrific!

I can say with confidence that the money you save will be substantial. It is not uncommon to routinely pay half of what other people do if you make the right decisions on when, where, and how you travel. I know because I've been watching it happen over and over for two decades now, no matter where I visit. As a travel writer who publishes books and articles on value travel, I pay close attention to prices and get as much information as I can from people I come in contact with along the way. When people tell me how much they're spending on their vacation, I just smile nicely and don't let on what my own expenses have been like. But if you feel the urge to gloat later, I'm not going to stop you.

WHAT TO EXPECT

In case you think I'm going to be a travel snob who is always going to look down his nose at popular destinations, chain hotels, and breakfast buffets, let me ease your mind. I've been to plenty of tourist magnets such as Cancun, London, Myrtle Beach, and Jamaica and had a blast. I've made trips to all-inclusive resorts and have probably spent a year's worth of nights in chain hotels. I've stayed at Ritz-Carltons and Club Meds, as well as Comfort Inns and Microtels. I've also traveled in the middle of high season and knowingly overpaid when I had to get somewhere in a hurry. I've paid a premium to be where I wanted to be on a special occasion. There's a time and a place for all these choices and any of them can certainly give you a great travel experience. I'm frugal, but I also know when to let go.

What I hope to get across, though, is that "the way it is done" is an option, not a given. You won't get sent to the principal's office for not following the norm. For the contrarian traveler, there's almost always a better value route. As I'll point out in the final chapter, there are times when you should just forget the price altogether and just do what you really want to do to make the experience special. This guide is for all the other times.

Like most writers on any subject, I have my own point of view and it's only fair to admit up front that I'm biased in some areas. I do tend to favor locally owned hotels and restaurants when I travel overseas. Yes, they're usually a better value, but I also repeatedly find I get a much stronger sense of place and meet a wider variety of people, including locals. I shy away from tightly scheduled group tours because I like to see things at my own pace. I don't like giving up control over how I spend my day and how much free time I have. I like to spend some real time in a place and see what it has to offer, so a one-day port stop doesn't cut it. In short, I like my options to be up to me, not someone in the travel industry.

If I seem to give short shrift to "Europe in Eight Days" tours or big Caribbean cruises, I hope you'll understand. Even if you love those kinds of trips, you'll still find plenty of advice in here that will help you shave costs. Just be aware that with these trips you have handed over much of the decision-making ability to someone else—someone who is getting a commission.

I could easily fill this book up with 1,000 very specific tips to save you money on travel, and probably another two or three books' worth more to make a trilogy of it. But that's monotonous for both of us and it's too much for anyone to digest. You will not see detailed checklists on what time of night to buy your plane ticket, which hotel chain currently offers the best breakfast, or which frequent-flyer program can earn you a free ticket the fastest. All these kinds of tips are fleeting and would be out of date before the ink dried on these pages. I'd rather share principles that are simpler and more permanent. Besides, there are always going to be plenty of web sites to check out for an update on the deals of the week.

For the same reason, I will only mention a specific web site if it is a true "category killer" as they say in the business world. Priceline.com qualifies. CheapTicketJoe.com does not. The really key sites mentioned in the text can be found at the resources section in the back. All the rest will be listed and continually updated on the accompanying web site www.ContrarianTraveler.com.

While I've certainly learned more in my years of globetrotting than I ever did in four years of college, this is not going to read like a textbook. Travel is supposed to be fun, no matter how or where you go, so reading about it should be fun, too. I hope you learn a lot, become a little wiser, and become inspired to travel more and travel better. Let's hit the road!

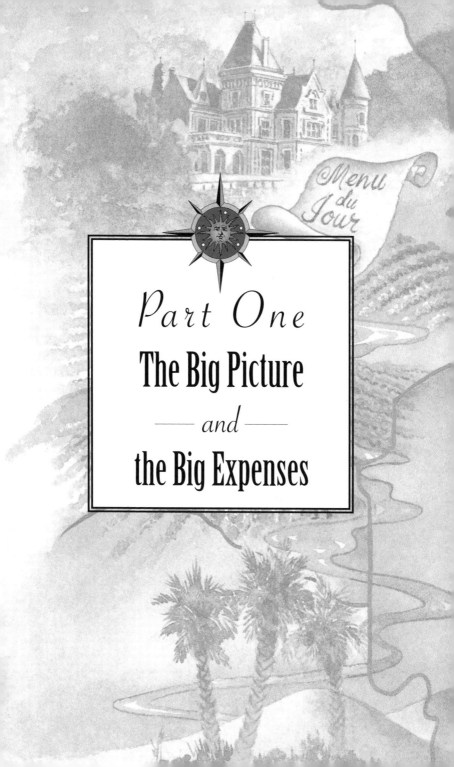

Part One
The Big Picture
— and —
the Big Expenses

WHY THE WORDS "TRAVEL" AND "EXPENSIVE" ARE SO INTERTWINED

Is Everyone Really Jetting Off to a Luxury Spa This Weekend?

"Tales of unforgettable encounters and soul-stretching adventures don't sell ads as well as tales of glitzy hotels and high-priced restaurants."

—Don George, Global Travel Editor, Lonely Planet Publishing

When Mr. and Mrs. Smith make vacation plans, they usually plan for "somewhere they've always wanted to go" and then look for a good deal. They usually find a nice package deal, plop down the money they have been saving up for a year, and spend a week in a nice resort, taking the occasional excursion on a group tour bus. On those occasions when they're taking a short trip for a long weekend, they decide when they want to go and book something online at one of the most popular web sites. They usually pay the prevailing rate, despite the time they spend searching for the best airfare deal. They return home to a depleted bank account or lots of credit card debt.

The Johnsons, on the other hand, know there's a better way. Before making plans, they look at which dates offer the best value and see if a mid-week departure will shave some money off their flight costs. They don't tie themselves to a specific destination, keeping their options open to where there's a good value. They choose a lesser-known independent hotel that is a better value than a cookie-cutter chain hotel. After arriving at their destination, they take advantage of local restaurants, local guides, and alternative transportation options. On those occasions when they're taking a trip for a short weekend, they wait until the last minute to find a bargain offer, using a last-minute travel site or buying something at a travel auction. They know they got the best deal possible and return home to a bank account still containing enough funds for their next trip.

Are you a Smith or a Johnson?

Let's first look at how you spend your money when you're not traveling. How do you shop for other things? When you spend non-travel money, do you like to pay top dollar, or do you try to find a bargain?

Few people are willing to pay list price when they open their wallet. A survey conducted by *Money Magazine* found that even among the wealthiest 25% of Americans, 92% said "they enjoy buying things more if they thought they got a bargain." A survey from Visa found that three-quarters of consumers who have at least $125,000 in household income clip coupons, and two-thirds shop at discount and warehouse stores.

Despite our innate desire to uncover a bargain, even the most frugal shoppers will often throw caution to the wind when they make travel plans. Someone who drives ten blocks to save five cents per gallon on gasoline will charge $3,000 for a family holiday on the credit card without hesitation. A couple who agonizes over whether to spend an extra $12 per month to have HBO on their TV will spend ten minutes or less discussing ways to save money on their next vacation. A guy who spends a whole day trying to research how to shave $200 off the price of a new car will then spend ten minutes researching the hotel where he will be spending a week.

Contrarian travelers do their homework and travel more or better as a result. Unlike the conformists who do what the travel marketers suggest, contrarian travelers know the game and know how to get around it. They shop for travel as carefully as they would shop for a car or a sofa and they take advantage of the fact that most people don't bother. By avoiding the herd mentality, they pay the full price only if they really feel that it is completely justified.

In my decades of travel in North America and abroad, I've seen plenty of travelers from both camps. I've circled the globe three times and spent at least a year out of the country each trip. One of the first questions most people would ask me and my wife was, "How in the world could you afford to travel for so long?" From their point of view, "travel" could only mean expensive hotels, rental cars, and meals in tourist restaurants. The fact we had routinely found nice beach bungalows with a bath for less than $10 a night was beyond their comprehension. Our tales of nice restaurant meals for less than $2 each were unfathomable. They couldn't imagine how you would get from country to country without spending a fortune.

The world most vacationers see is far different from the world seen by contrarian travelers. For instance:

- You don't have to spend $200+ per night on a hotel to have a nice room and enjoy your trip.

- There are plenty of transportation options beyond rental cars and group tour buses.

- Eating where the locals eat is not only cheaper, it's usually better.

- A good vacation doesn't have to mean staying in a sequestered resort with other sequestered tourists.

- Local costs at your destination don't have to match what you'd spend at home.

- You don't necessarily have to be some place when everyone else is also there.

In other words, the way most people take for granted as "how it's done" is quite opposite of the way those who are in control of their budget think it's done. As a result, the contrarian traveler is like the proverbial seatmate who is paying half what you did for his airfare, except he is also paying less for hotels, transportation, meals, and souvenirs.

In order to understand why the contrarian traveler is able to consistently get better deals, we have to look at why the typical traveler does what he or she does. For some background, here's a brief tutorial on how the travel industry works. Trust me when I say this section will be brief and informative. The last thing I want to do is bore you to death with an economics lecture in the very first chapter. To understand how to make money-saving decisions though, you have to understand why it is much easier to make bad ones.

THE GREAT TRAVEL MEDIA MACHINE

Let's start with a short exercise. Off the top of your head, name the last three travel magazines or travel newspaper sections you read.

Done? Now, think hard and try to remember how many articles you saw about traveling on a tight budget.

Those two answers probably sum up everything you need to know about why people travel the way they do. *Arthur Frommer's Budget Travel* has done a good job of showing the mainstream reader how to get a better deal, but its circulation is dwarfed by that of *Travel + Leisure* and *Condé Nast Traveler*, magazines that are really aimed at the most affluent citizens of the world's most affluent country. Big city newspapers such as *The New York Times* and the *Chicago Tribune* contain some great travel writing, but only a fraction of the typical Sunday travel section pays more than passing attention to finding the best values. When they do give a nod to value, their "bargain" tips usually focus on how to get a $400 hotel for $250, or how to get a package deal to Fiji for less than $2,000. This was true even during the travel slump and recession of the early 2000s. You see lots of luxury, luxury, luxury, as if every couple boarding a plane is on their way to a five-star hotel and spa treatment. Over time, this warps readers' perceptions and makes them think every vacation has to cost a fortune.

A travel writer I know calls these luxury publications "travel porn" and I can't think of a more apt description. I once saw a cartoon in a men's magazine in which a woman is standing next to a pot-bellied man in an easy chair. "Why do you watch that stuff?" the woman asks, pointing to a pornographic movie playing on the TV. "Because it makes me feel like everyone in the world is having a wild and crazy time," he replies. "Well, everyone except me."

The idea of fantasizing about a life you can't lead yourself is a big part of the "armchair traveler" appeal of glossy travel magazines. A typical issue contains dozens of advertisements for diamond watches, luxury sports cars, and handbags that retail for over a thousand dollars. Between the ads are stories about resorts we can only dream of frequenting unless we're in that lofty portion of the population who has far more money than time.

It's nice to look at the pretty pictures and read about lounging in luxury spas in the Maldives if that's as far as it goes. For too many non-millionaire tourists, however, they look at those stories and think that's how everyone travels—everyone except them. So when they pick up the phone or log on to make travel reservations, they go in with the mindset that travel is, and should be, expensive.

As a society we get more aspirational each year. A study done by Harvard found that money does buy happiness, but only if you have more of it than your neighbors. So those caught up in the "affluenza" cycle build bigger houses, buy more expensive cars, and travel like the luxury magazines tell them they should be traveling—whether they can afford it or not. Instead of the purpose of a vacation being renewal, education, experience, or inspiration, it becomes just another way for the Smiths to keep up with their neighbors.

Why does this happen?

In part, this happens because the bigger and better funded the tourism marketing and PR organization is, the better chance it has of getting its story into print. Most magazine editors probably don't consciously pick stories to please advertisers, but you often see an eerie correlation over time between the subject of advertisements and the subject of stories. (Sometimes the two even join, in the "special advertising supplement" that is meant to look like the magazine's editorial—except for the small print disclosure at the top of the page.) If you don't believe me, go to the library and pull out the last half-dozen issues of one of these magazines. Then count the articles and ads for European cities, Caribbean beaches, spas, ski resorts, and fancy adventure tours.

The more a vacation costs, the more likely that resort or tour company has an ample marketing budget. It's all about the quantity and quality of visitors. If more people come, that drives up revenue. If those people spend more on high-end lodging and services, that improves "margin." Margin is the spread between cost and revenue, leading to gross or net profit. Nearly any business owner would prefer to sell high-margin goods or services over low-margin ones. Automobile companies don't push all-wheel drive as an option because we each live on snowy hillsides: it's because the profit margin on these systems is 40% (versus 26% for a sunroof and 12% for a full spare tire). That clerk at Best Buy is not trying to sell you an extended warranty because he is concerned about your future happiness: it's because those warranties are four or five times more profitable than the actual electronics in your shopping cart.

High margins are a key factor in tourism marketing. It's why very few magazines for budget travelers survive over time. There are plenty of budget travelers who are voracious readers, but the advertisers don't care about reaching them. They would rather reach the aspirational traveler who spends freely and will contribute a lot to the bottom line in a hurry.

Well-funded tourism organizations are more likely to sponsor press junkets for writers. I'll admit I've been on a few of them myself. Travel writers are notoriously under-paid, so most can't go do a story on Patagonian horse ranch-es or a two-week trek through some new and remote

Shangri-La unless a sponsor is helping with expenses. There's a whole sub-industry that matches up travel writers with public relations firms and tourism bureaus, with annual conferences, several newsletters, and dedicated web sites.

If a fancy resort puts up Susie the travel writer and wines and dines her for a few nights, she is not nearly as likely to go check out Hal's Hammock Hideaway down the beach, even if it is a better value. She may not even get much time to go exploring, so she won't see many of the restaurants and bars where the locals hang out. The biggest magazines like to brag that their writers don't take sponsored trips, but that only means the magazine is paying all expenses instead, usually at a negotiated discount rate. So the writer still doesn't have any incentive to find the best values.

As in many industries, whoever spends the most on publicity typically gets the most press coverage. It's not sinister and it's not underhanded, but it is something most tourists don't understand or think about. If you see twelve stories next year about some lake resort in Switzerland, no, it doesn't mean there's some big trend you somehow missed out on. It doesn't mean that region is heaven on earth and your local lake region down the road is just ho-hum. It only means the former has some talented people and ample resources in their visitors' bureau.

After all these stories and ads hit, more people go there, then the resort or tourism agency has more money to spend, which results in more press and advertising, which results in more people going there. Then there's even more press from the magazines and newspapers that don't allow writers to go on sponsored trips because "it's the happening place to go right now." The circle continues to spiral up until some catastrophe hits and everyone stops going. (Then the contrarian traveler moves in to take advantage of the price drops. See Chapter 2 for more on this strategy.)

The system works very well for everyone involved. The Smiths and everyone like them take the bait—hook, line, and sinker. The Johnsons keep on swimming.

Yes, some wealthy people want fantastic service and the most plush surroundings all the time. They're willing to pay whatever it costs to be pampered 24/7. They'll buy and develop their own island if they have to. But I'm guessing that if you picked up this book, you're not one of them. Even if you travel in style, you're probably not willing to pay a week's wages for a hotel room just because the place offers a pillow menu and sheets with a high thread count. You're not going to go somewhere just because a magazine cover says it's where all the fashionable people are going this year. You want to make sure your money is getting you a good value, whether you are spending $5 or $500.

Next time you leaf through a travel magazine, take a look at the non-travel advertisements. Do those products match up with the way you live your life? If not, try a different magazine—and a different kind of travel. For a list of travel magazines that are based on a more realistic view and budget, see the Resources section at the end of the book.

THE GREAT TRAVEL MARKETING MACHINE

Now it's time for the next quiz. Quickly:

> *Name the first three Caribbean islands that pop into your head.*
> *Name a South Pacific island with nice beaches.*
> *Name two nice destinations in Mexico.*
> *Name a place you'd like to visit in South America.*

Now, why those particular answers? What made you think of those countries or cities?

Whether you want to admit it or not, you were probably influenced by good marketing or good public relations. Places such as Fiji, Tahiti, Jamaica, and the Bahamas have very well-oiled marketing machines, both collectively as a tourism board and individually as attractions and hotel chains. Cancun, Mexico is perhaps the world's greatest example of a government turning a once-deserted stretch of beach into a hugely popular resort area. Brazil has made Rio de Janeiro roll off the world's tongue and Peru has done a great job of making the Machu Picchu ruins near Cusco a must-see. If any of these were in your answers, it's no accident.

Tourism is often estimated to be the biggest industry in the world. It's also growing at a healthy clip. As the world's middle class gets larger, more people travel. As more people retire with ample bank accounts, they can afford more trips. As air connections increase and roads get better, it becomes easier to get around more areas. Just as the number of travelers increases, however, so does the number of businesses trying to get a piece of that action. As a result, competition is intense and will probably continue to be more intense in the future.

Just a few decades ago, some of the world's capitals had only one or two international hotels. Hilton didn't have to try too hard to woo visitors in many of these places: they were the only game in town. If you wanted to do business in some other cities, you flew on Pan Am and stayed at the InterContinental: you didn't have any other choice. Very few travelers, apart from hardy backpackers, went to Thailand, Turkey, or Morocco because there were few facilities for visitors in these "exotic" locations. In the U.S., you will find few hotels in any medium-sized city that have been around more than fifty years.

Those days are gone and the stakes have gotten higher. Even tiny Laos has a significant marketing budget. Hotel chains have a giant international war chest to work with. The word "branding" is thrown around in tourism meetings the same way it is at Coca-Cola or Proctor & Gamble. I've heard more than one tourism bureau official speak of their "product array." These marketing teams are trying to hit you at multiple points of contact: on your TV, in your magazines, in your newspaper, and on the web. They even buy your loyalty with airline and hotel points you can redeem for awards. You can run, but you can't hide.

Popularity breeds popularity and the most-visited destinations wield tremendous clout. The continent of Europe gets an incredible 57% of international travelers, according to the World Travel Organization. Even if you back out the Europeans crossing borders to visit another country, that's still an amazing market share. France alone gets over 75 million visitors per year. When European countries want to market their attractions, they're certainly not doing it on a shoestring.

The following table is a bit skewed by business travelers (thus the high rankings for China and Japan), but it gives a general view of where U.S. travelers are headed. If you've always wanted to visit England or France, but couldn't put your finger on why, it's probably because you'd be joining plenty of other travelers who head that way each year. That kind of traffic pays for a lot of advertising and public relations campaigns (and creates a lot of envious neighbors in American towns).

TOP INTERNATIONAL DESTINATIONS FOR
AMERICAN TRAVELERS

Rank	Country	Travelers
1	Mexico	19.36 million
2	Canada	15.06 million
3	United Kingdom	3.69 million
4	France	2.41 million
5	Italy	1.92 million
6	China	1.81 million
7	Germany	1.75 million
8	Jamaica	1.26 million
9	Japan	1.07 million
10	Bahamas	1.01 million

Source: U.S. Department of Commerce, ITA

There's nothing inherently wrong with marketing or PR. Every organization has to get its message out somehow or it will go out of business. Marketing alone cannot sustain popularity anyway: if nobody has fun at a specific destination, all the marketing in the world won't help. I've got nothing against heavily marketed places such as Jamaica, Miami, or London; I've had a great time in all three and will gladly go back again. I've also stayed in some stunning international chain hotels that I didn't want to leave. Just understand the motivation for everyone showing up at these same places at the same time. Understand why "everyone is going there," and realize that this is likely a result of a talented or well-funded marketing team. Then think about maybe heading somewhere else, or at least going when it's not high season. You'll probably save a fortune in the process.

The Great Travel Lodging Machine

If you usually stay at a well-known hotel, you're certainly not alone.

Starwood Hotels & Resorts is a company worth over $7 billion, with some 850 hotels in 80 countries. You probably know their properties well: Sheraton, St. Regis, Le Meridien, Four Points, Westin, and W.

Hilton has over 2,800 properties worldwide, in 80 countries. This conglomerate includes Doubletree, Hampton Inns, Embassy Suites, Homewood Suites, and Conrad.

The InterContinental Hotels Group has over 3,300 hotels across 100 countries, including various Holiday Inn brands, Crowne Plaza, Staybridge Suites, and Candlewood Suites.

Marriott is worth over $10 billion and runs over 2,500 properties under the brands of Marriott, J.W. Marriott, Ritz-Carlton, Renaissance, Ramada, Residence Inn, and Fairfield Inn.

Privately owned Hyatt has 207 properties in 39 countries.

In the Caribbean, SuperClubs owns the Starfish, SuperClubs Breezes, and Grand Lido properties.

Occidental Hotels has 80 hotels in 13 countries under the brands of Allegro, Grand, and Occidental.

Then there's Club Med, Sandals, and a half-dozen others who control a large number of the big resorts.

Right about now, you're probably saying, "Ummm, who cares?" Well, in the end, it probably doesn't matter who owns what when it comes to your own vacation, but just realize that there's a good reason these chains have great name recognition. They've paid for it. You'll have a tough time opening a Sunday paper or a travel magazine without seeing their ads or seeing stories mentioning one of their properties. If you travel much, you probably get junk mail from one or all of them. Their ads pop up on your computer screen and you can't go to a booking site without running across them again.

But does every hotel stay have to cost the published rates that these companies are charging? No way. Pick up a guidebook, pull up some of the web sites listed in this book, or ask around for suggestions. There are a lot of other options out there, often representing an equal or better value. Chapter 5 will cover specific strategies for getting the best lodging deal every time.

THE GREAT TRAVEL BOOKING MACHINE

Since the dawn of the internet, the way we book vacations has gone through a radical change. We consumers have become far more empowered and are able to weigh decisions based on a wide variety of information, not just on what a travel agent tells us. We can go online and read hotel reviews, see photos of a resort, check airline on-time records, and even find out what other people have paid for their tickets or rooms through Priceline.

Despite all this power, we are still pushed toward the highest-priced options and the most sterile forms of vacations, especially if we're in a hurry. Again, it's not some evil conspiracy—it's just business. Large airlines, large hotel chains, and large vacation tour companies have the most marketing muscle. They're able to form partnerships, place big ads, and give incentives to agents (including online ones) to push their products. IAC Travel, a company you have probably never heard of, controls a full half of the online booking market in the U.S. They own Expedia, Hotels.com, Hotwire, and TripAdvisor.

Try a little experiment on your computer when you get some time. Pull up Expedia, Travelocity, or Orbitz and try to find info on little family-owned inns, places with fewer than thirty rooms. See what you can learn about public transportation where you're headed. Try to find out what it would cost to fly on Taca, Southwest, SpiritAir, EasyJet, or Lan Chile. Don't feel bad if you strike out; you're not meant to succeed on any of these counts. Most travel agents aren't interested in these unprofitable options and neither are their Internet equivalents. You'll have to hunt down the real bargains yourself—and be sure you are getting the whole story when you do find a deal.

The Muddy Window of Pricing on the Web
by Ed Perkins

When I first started looking at travel from a consumer perspective, I found lots of "inside" stories to tell. Knowledge of airline consolidators was confined to a small minority of travelers— usually, an ethnic minority. Hardly anybody knew how to score a discount on a hotel room, beyond a minor 10% senior or AAA discount. But the last twenty years have seen a sea change. More consumer travel journalists started to report the truth, not just what advertisers wanted, and the internet made virtually the entire marketplace transparent to anyone willing to spend the time investigating it. As a result, the industry has almost no "secret" deals any more. No secrets, however, doesn't mean nothing to report. The industry still bends—and occasionally breaks—the truth in its advertising.

Currently, one of the travel industry's most prevalent marketing scams is what I call "split" pricing. That means featuring a price, in big type, that is less than the full price you actually have to pay. Suppliers who play that game arbitrarily divide the true price into two or more pieces, feature just one of them in big type (and in the prices they submit to online comparison sites), then add in the other only after you've done your price comparisons and are well into the buying process.

Take European hotels, for example. In Europe, they're required to include the VAT (value-added tax) as part of the advertised price. But when they advertise in the U.S. (and list rates on the internet), some deduct the VAT from the headline price, while other more honest competitors don't. Result: a price comparison distorted by as much as 25%.

A few years back, most of the big cruise lines highlighted a low-ball price, then added in "port charges" that puffed the real price by 20-30%. While the big lines stopped doing that (thanks to the Florida Attorney General), some independent cruise agencies still do.

Some hotels add in "energy surcharges" or "resort fees" as separate add-ons instead of including them in the advertised price, as they should. A rental car pitched at $30 a day can cost more than $60 after all the extras. The list goes on and on.

One of the favorite tricks of split-pricing scamsters is to put a plausible sounding label on the part they exclude from the featured price, such as "taxes and service" or "port charges." Those labels are plausible because governments actually do pile charge after charge on the travel industry. But the total of "taxes and service" is often considerably higher than the actual taxes required by governments, with the difference going to the supplier.

A related minor scam is including extras you may not want as "defaults" in the buying process: You automatically get hit with them unless you specifically decline. Default insurance charges, for example, are fairly prevalent when you buy a package tour or an air-hotel combo.

The pervasive power of the internet, if anything, increases the pressure on suppliers to resort to split pricing (and other scams). Since their price figures and their competitors' figures are out there for everyone to see—and compare—they resort to finagling.

Some internet comparison sites have tried to even out the playing field. All three of the biggest—Expedia, Orbitz, and Travelocity—give you the option to look at the "total cost" of a car rental, including all the extra fees. That approach makes split pricing virtually impossible. Sadly, however, those sites aren't making the same effort for airfares or hotel rates.

The result? Even with its supposed transparency, the internet is still full of pitfalls for the unwary. A combination of knowledge, skepticism, and vigilance is as important as it ever was.

Ed Perkins is a columnist for SmarterTravel.com, the founder of Consumer Reports Travel Letter, *and the author of several books, including* Business Travel When It's Your Money.

When the Smiths purchase a one-week vacation package to an all-inclusive resort, everybody in the food chain gets a piece of a nice profit margin. Money flows to the resort, the company that transports them to the hotel, the airline, the agency where they booked it, the local government receiving the luxury room tax, and even the newspaper where the Smiths saw that full-page ad for the package. Extras like trip insurance get thrown into the mix without most people even noticing. It's a nice system for everyone involved in the partnership: revenues are predictable, the cross-marketing ensures a steady stream of customers, and everyone can be herded into charter planes and group tour buses.

Now let's imagine that the Johnsons follow a more independent path and book it all on their own. They buy a last-minute flight from a discounter and split their seven nights between a resort they booked on an auction site and a small local inn they found in their guidebook. They take local transportation, including a public shuttle from the airport. They eat at a variety of local restaurants, depending on what they're in the mood for or where they happen to be. If they want to visit some ruins on the outskirts somewhere, they get there on their own instead of in a packaged excursion. In the end, they've spent a fraction of what the Smiths did.

Lots of people still made money off the Johnsons, but with fragmented providers, there was no coordinated marketing effort. There were no projected earnings that a corporation could plot on a graph. Big-league travel marketers don't like this: the Johnsons are too hard to influence and there's less revenue to spread around. It's all too unpredictable to track and build a quarterly business plan around. The more partnerships that are involved in a transaction, the more likely you're being pushed down the most predictable and profitable path.

Does this mean an all-inclusive package deal is a bad deal? No, and as I'll stress in the last chapter, you always have to take the time and effort to pull out a calculator. Many of these package deals employ charter flights, so the airfare portion is less than a commercial flight through a common carrier would cost. Since hotel rooms are booked at group rates, the whole package is often cheaper than something a couple could line up on their own. Illogical as it seems, sometimes it's cheaper to buy the lowest-priced package deal and throw away some of the hotel room nights just to get the cheaper airfare. Other times, however, especially outside high season, this is not the case.

It also makes sense to book a packaged adventure tour through a reputable company if your time is limited and you want to have everything taken care of in advance. Or if all you really want to do is sit on a beach and keep the cocktails flowing, it can make sense to just book it all in five minutes and go. I'll cover these kinds of exceptions in more detail at the end of the book.

Travel Industry Questions for the Contrarian Traveler

1. *Why are you choosing the destination you are choosing? Is there a specific reason you're going there, such as a stunning sight or adventure activity, or is there just some nagging feeling that "it's the place to go"?*

2. *Are you basing your decision on what will sound impressive when you tell your friends and neighbors, or are you basing it on where you think you'll have the most fun on your existing budget?*

3. *Do you want to stay in a hotel room that looks the same in Cleveland or Cairo, with all of the same attributes as one at home, or would you like to stay in a place with some local*

flavor? Is there a good reason you're choosing a corporate chain hotel, or is it just a reflex purchase?

4. *Are you choosing a pre-planned vacation package because it's a good deal, or because you're going somewhere remote where you're dependent on professional guides? Or are you just choosing that path because it doesn't require making decisions?*

2

CONTRARIAN DESTINATIONS

Countries on Sale, Substitutions, and the CNN Effect

"Dismiss common sense. Leave the herd for a while."
—Bruce Northam, *Globetrotter Dogma*

When the Smiths decide where to go on vacation, they start by picking out their destination, then base their budget on whatever the costs are like for that particular area. If it's more than they expected, they take their lumps and pay more. The Johnsons, on the other hand, figure out what they're looking to do or see, then find a good value that fits the bill. They never have a problem sticking to their original budget.

The Johnsons know that their choice of destination can have a bigger impact on their budget than any travel decision they make. This is true whether they are taking a break for a long weekend or are figuring out an itinerary for an around-the-world journey that will last for a year.

To put things in perspective, let's look at the published price of a midweek double room at the Hyatt in various locations in North America and abroad.

STANDARD DOUBLE ROOM, HYATT HOTEL IN VARIOUS CITIES

City	Published Double Room Rate in US Dollars
New York, USA	$389
Istanbul, Turkey	$239
Toronto, Canada	$285
Tokyo, Japan	$470
Mérida, Mexico	$119
Caymen Islands	$349
Kathmandu, Nepal	$100
Milan, Italy	$650
Austin, USA	$150

Source: Hyatt.com

Regardless of what you spend on airfare, a trip to Milan, the Caymen Islands, or Tokyo is going to cost far more than a trip to anywhere else on the list. *The Wall Street Journal* publishes a rundown each week with the average hotel prices for business travelers in U.S. cities. The top entry is invariably New York City, usually topping $300 per night. Boston or Washington D.C. is generally next, at around $250 to $300. Other cities vary wildly and give you a good idea of where the bargains are. Chicago and Houston come in at around $180. The average is less than $150 in Miami, Orlando, Atlanta, Minneapolis, Denver, and Phoenix.

These are deluxe hotels, which have far less variance than mid-range hotels. If we looked at equivalents to a three-star hotel or a bed-and-breakfast hotel, the differences would be even more dramatic. Internationally, you would also find even bigger differences in the things that the locals purchase every day: simple restaurant meals, groceries, subway fare, or a bus or train to the next city. (Crossing the country on a coach class bullet train in Japan costs five times the rate for a first-class train all the way from Singapore to Bangkok, Thailand, even though the latter is 500 miles farther.)

When you travel to a cheaper destination, nearly everything you spend money on is cheaper. According to the company publishing the Zagat Guides, the average price for a meal in New York City, across the board, is close to $38 per person. Any Western European capital will be comparable or higher. In Cusco, Peru, that figure is probably around $6. In Bangkok, Thailand, it's probably $3. The average could easily slide close to a buck in wide swaths of Laos, Indonesia, Nepal, or India.

Next time you flip through a major magazine or travel section of a newspaper, study the prices for restaurants highlighted in the details. Even between various U.S. cities—say Chicago and Austin—the contrast can be striking. Internationally, however, it's amplified. In one magazine I looked at as I was putting this chapter together, a hotspot in Bangkok required a total of $15 for a couple's dinner. One of the fanciest restaurants in Istanbul came with a dinner tab of $50 for two. At a comparable restaurant in Rome, the tab was $195—for *lunch*!

At times, you won't have a choice about where you are going. There are relatives to visit, a wedding to go to, friends to compromise with, or maybe a timeshare you're locked into visiting during a certain week of the year. When you do have a choice, however, make the absolute most of it. If your choices are very narrow, your pricing power is limited. If you're flexible on where you go, however, you can easily save hundreds of dollars in a weekend, or save enough money in one week to take a whole other trip. Some places somewhere will be "on sale," no matter when you're going.

How do you decide where to go on vacation?

The answer can vary a lot between different people. Once you get beyond the obligatory trips, where to next? If you're a typical American, chances are you're staying in the U.S. or are heading to Western Europe, the Caribbean, or the beaches of Mexico. Or maybe Canada. But there's a big world out there beyond those choices, and most of them are a better value. Even within those limited areas, costs can vary dramatically from place to place. Imagine the price differences between Nashville and New York, between the Dominican Republic and the British Virgin Islands, or between Zurich and Budapest.

Throughout this chapter, we'll look at the macro to micro decisions that can affect prices. We'll look at the selection of countries, areas within a country, and even how different sections of a city can have a major impact on your budget. This assumes, of course, that you're calling your own shots. Most people who choose an organized tour will give up control over at least two of these three options. If the group tour prices are low enough to offset this drawback, and you don't mind having your time scheduled by someone else, then the tour can still be a good deal. Many times this is not true, however, so it's important to pull out a calculator and compare. With prices as transparent as they are today on the web, it is easier than ever to do the math.

We'll also look at the most common destinations and examine alternatives that can cut your vacation costs in half. The aim is to have a similar or richer experience, but on a fraction of the budget. By literally heading a different direction than the herds are going, you'll profit from the lack of competition.

Lastly, we'll examine some of the unfounded fears that keep travelers from getting a better value. When you are finished with this chapter, you will be armed with information necessary to help you find the best destination values.

LOCAL CHOICES—CITY BLOCKS AND ALTERNATE BEACHES

In the not-so-distant past, travelers left most choices up to their travel agent, especially for trips out of the country. It took a lot of effort to figure out where city hotels were in relation to subways and museums and there were few ways to make head-to-head comparisons. It took hours to pore through guidebooks, maps in hand. Making reservations in foreign countries was a major pain. All that has changed. From the comfort of your computer chair, you can now figure all this out yourself with a few clicks of the mouse. If you do have a good guidebook in hand at the same time (often available to check out from your local library), you will have more information at your fingertips than most agents did a decade ago. By taking advantage of these tools, you can easily take control of your expenses.

"Location, location, location" applies to real estate, and therefore to hotels and restaurants as well. By just moving a few blocks away, or by staying in a less ritzy or less popular area, you can often cut your hotel and restaurant costs by a third or more. You see this clearly in large cities throughout the world, where the "downtown" or prime business district is the area with the highest rates. Most of the people buying hotel rooms and restaurant meals in these areas are relying on company expense accounts, so anyone paying out of his or her own pocket will feel a sting. For instance, it is much harder to find bargains in the midtown area of New York City than it is in the rest of Manhattan. The phrase "tourist trap" definitely applies: you won't find locals eating dinner out in this area unless they're grabbing a bite after work or going to the theater.

If you're heading to Washington D.C., you might want to think twice about staying near the White House and Smithsonian. You'll pay quite a premium to be right in the thick of the action and you are competing with well-funded lobbyists. Stay a few subway stops away, however, and the price drops dramatically. Even getting one block off the main drag saved us a small fortune on a peak weekend in Las Vegas. The same principle applies to many international locations, from Prague to Sydney to Tokyo. The exception to this is a short weekend stay, when business area hotels are sharply discounted. (You may still get hit hard on parking and restaurant rates, however, and find many restaurants closed or empty.)

In other areas, it is important to do some research and find out what the true costs will be. A guidebook alone is a great help. In some large cities, a good subway system can open up your options considerably. In others, you're at the mercy of taxis. In Cairo, for example, it may sound romantic to be out by the pyramids in Giza, but you'll be far away from the city's other attractions and will do a lot of haggling with opportunistic taxi drivers. In Bangkok, what looks close on the map can actually take an hour in the snarled traffic. The Las Vegas strip looks deceptively easy to cover on foot, when in fact it is over four miles long. In London or Manhattan, however, it's hard to go wrong if you're anywhere near a tube/subway stop.

Take advantage of overbuilding, however, when it creates brutal competition. Las Vegas is seldom hurting for visitors, but there are nearly always more rooms than patrons. Especially midweek, you can find great deals at quality properties. The same is true in many other cities, from Orlando to Nashville and Bangkok to Bali. When this is the case, compare prices and see what makes sense; you can often be right where you want to be, but at a rate as good as less convenient locations.

If you're going to splash out at some all-inclusive beach resort, then by all means get something on the ocean. But do you really need or want to be right in the thick of things? Often a resort a few miles away from the main drag will have more space and will be priced much lower. Or a resort with 200 rooms instead of 2,000 may be priced lower and won't be so spread out. A savings of $40-$50 per night will pay for a lot of cab rides to the nightlife.

If you're renting a house or villa for a week or two in some beach town, is it really worth the premium to be right on top of the waves? (In many cases, your walk from a block away is closer than the hike from the guestrooms at many "oceanfront" resorts.) You can often get a bigger house or a much better rate if you open up your options a bit wider. Rental house prices drop as much as half when there is no water view.

This all assumes you're making reservations. If you're not, you'll probably be relying on your guidebook, the advice of other travelers, and practical considerations such as proximity to the train or bus station. In some international cities, there's a defined budget travel zone where most of the cheap options are located. This area will also have the backpacker eateries, money-changers, travel agents that specialize in rock-bottom airfares, and shops selling used books. In cases like this, it doesn't make much sense to venture too far away because it can be hard to get your errands taken care of quickly. Just show up, take a look around, and pick the place you like best for the price. If there is sufficient competition, a budget hotel's price will mainly be determined by market forces, including long-term popularity.

OTHER PARTS OF THE COUNTRY

Some parts of a country are deluged with tourists, while you could have other parts all to yourself. The Czech Republic is one of the most polarized examples: some 80% of the country's visitors spend every night in Prague. As a result, lodging prices in Prague are nearly as high as they are in Western Europe. Venture an hour away, however, and rates drop by 50% or more.

In the United States, the most congested tourist traffic areas, according to AAA, are no surprise. They include Cape Cod, the Jersey Shore, the Outer Banks of North Carolina, Lake Tahoe (Nevada), Myrtle Beach (South Carolina), Branson (Missouri), and Napa Valley (California).

Mexico is a very large country, yet the top five resort areas pull in nearly all of the foreign visitors. For many travelers, huge Brazil means only one place: Rio de Janeiro. Argentina is just Buenos Aires. The Netherlands means Amsterdam (with maybe a quick day trip to some windmills and a cheese factory). You can apply the same rule of thumb to many "greatest hits of travel": London, Paris, Rome/Florence, Barcelona, and Beijing.

Because of this, most travelers come away with a very warped impression of a country. Imagine basing your opinion of the USA on one visit to New York City or Los Angeles. Or thinking all of Canada was like Toronto. Visiting the main destination in a country is also one of the easiest ways to drain your wallet. Look at the difference in cost between a week in San Francisco and a week in any small town in Middle America. That same striking disparity plays out across the world. Urban centers are generally more expensive. Popular resort areas are also more costly, especially if patronized by lots of Americans, Europeans, or Japanese.

Any "hot" place being written up in the glossy travel magazines is usually expensive or is getting that way fast. As mentioned in Chapter 1, bargain-priced places don't spend much on ads or trips for travel writers. A destination usually gets covered by the major travel magazines about the time when the first luxury hotel opens up. When a place is "hot," everything will be priced at a rate the tourists will bear, even if this is five or ten times what a local resident or budget traveler would pay.

The Other Side of the Island
by David Stanley

Although Fiji is one of the least expensive South Pacific countries, it's quite easy to spend a lot. The tariffs at exclusive boutique resorts like Turtle Island can run as high as US$3,000 a night per couple all-inclusive, and even family-oriented places like Castaway Island charge around $400 without meals. Add scuba diving at $75 a plunge and you're talking real money.

Tourists arriving at Fiji's Nadi International Airport are besieged by tour touts the moment they exit Immigration. The airport reps collect 30% commissions to send people to resorts in the Yasawa and Mamanuca groups west of Nadi, so they're always eager to make a sale. What the touts won't tell you is that you can have a comparable travel experience at a fraction the cost if you head east instead of west.

No one at Nadi Airport will mention the Cathay Hotels chain (www.fiji4less.com) because Cathay doesn't pay travel agent commissions. Instead, their business is generated through word-of-mouth advertising from travelers who have stayed at their five properties in Fiji. For example, Tubakula Beach Resort on the Coral Coast, right next to the fancy Outrigger Reef Resort, is a two-hour public bus ride southeast of Nadi Airport. The finest beachfront bungalows at Tubakula cost a quarter what the packaged tourists at the Outrigger are paying.

In Fiji's capital Suva, Cathay operates the popular South Seas Private Hotel, just up from the Botanical Gardens. Here the best double room is under $50, and a bed in the dorm is just $10. After a few days of city sightseeing and nightlife, the adventurous traveler will be ready to travel further east.

A top choice would be to take a ferry or fly to Fiji's first capital Levuka, on Ovalau Island, just northeast of Suva. Levuka hasn't changed much in over a century, and luckily, Ovalau doesn't have a good beach, so there aren't any flashy tourist resorts. What you will find here is Fiji's oldest and most atmospheric hotel and a string of intriguing historic sites. The hiking, dive shop, and Chinese restaurants are all great. Two old colonial clubs in Levuka serve visitors big bottles of Fiji Bitter.

The true adventurer could also elect to board a copra boat for the seldom-visited Lau Group on the eastern edge of Fiji, a two-day voyage from Suva. Or one can fly directly to Vanua Balavu Island in about an hour. A small backpacker resort called Moana's Guest House provides room and board in Vanua Balavu's largest village, Lomaloma, population 400. Swimming, hiking, exploring, and socializing are the main pursuits here.

Another option would be to take one of the regular car ferries from Suva to Vanua Levu or Taveuni islands in northern Fiji. Though expensive resorts do exist on those islands, there's still a lot to see and do for the independent budget traveler. The only thing you won't encounter is the main mass of tourists, which has been booked into hotels and resorts of western Fiji.

David Stanley is the author of many guidebooks, including Moon Handbooks South Pacific (www.southpacific.org) published by Avalon Travel Publishing. His South Pacific travel photos can be viewed on www.pacific-pictures.com.

You can stay in a "feels-like-home" resort in Cabo San Lucas for $300 per night, or you can go an hour up the coast and land in a real Mexican paradise for a third of that price. You can easily spend a fortune renting a house in popular Nags Head, North Carolina, or you can try a quieter spot on the Outer Banks coast and get far more house for your money. You can go skiing in Aspen or Jackson Hole and mingle with millionaires, or go to sleepier Rockies ski towns instead and ski the same powder for less. Or head to the Canadian Rockies and knock off another 20% at least.

ALTERNATIVE COUNTRIES

After spending a few years traveling around the world, I published a slim book called *The World's Cheapest Destinations: 21 Countries Where Your Dollars are Worth a Fortune*. My main motivation for writing it was to show people that there are plenty of countries in the world where your own currency can really go a long way. You can visit places where one dollar will get you two pints of beer in a pub or cover a sit-down meal. There are countries where $5 will get you a basic beach bungalow or a half-hour massage. There are places where $20-$30 will get you a car and driver for the day or a hotel with room service, a bellboy, and a pool.

The book has sold pretty well and has gotten some nice reviews, but even more encouraging have been the e-mails I get from travelers. One U.S. reader said, "I was extremely worried about my travel budget before I got your book. Now I am relieved and excited. I had no idea there were so many places you can travel to for a minimal cost."

This is not unusual. We're programmed to think travel has to be expensive, when in fact it can be cheaper than staying home.

21 OF THE BEST INTERNATIONAL TRAVEL VALUES

Americas	Europe	Middle East and Africa	Asia
Argentina	Turkey	Jordan	Thailand
Guatemala	Hungary	Egypt	Malaysia
Honduras	Bulgaria	Morocco	Laos
Nicaragua	Romania		Vietnam
Ecuador			Indonesia
Bolivia			India
Peru			Nepal

Source: The World's Cheapest Destinations

Visiting the great bargains of the world doesn't mean settling for less. Some of the world's greatest attractions are in some of the world's cheapest countries. You can see the great monuments you've read about since you were a child: the Taj Mahal, the Great Pyramids, the fantastic structures of the Incas and Mayans. You can explore some of the greatest jungles, hike in the highest mountains, and go rafting on the fastest whitewater rivers. You can visit some of the best dive and snorkeling spots on the planet. You'll also encounter unique cultures and see architecture unlike any you've ever experienced. But this requires breaking out of the usual patterns.

BEYOND WESTERN EUROPE

There are great values scattered throughout the world, both near and far. So why does seemingly everyone dream of going to Western Europe, one of the most expensive and tourist-deluged spots on the planet? For some people, maybe it's in their ancestral blood—the homeland calling and all that. Perhaps our educational system influences our subconscious, with all the time we spend on European history, music, and art. Or maybe some see it as just something you have to do before you die: you must see London, Paris, and Rome or you haven't really gone abroad.

Whatever the motivation, it's a costly proposition. When the U.S. dollar is strong, Europe is expensive. When the dollar is weak, a visit to Europe inspires frustrated shouts of "What the &#*% happened to all my money?!" You can always shave the air and hotel portions by going in the shoulder season (more on that in Chapter 3), but you'll still be gasping at the prices for taxis, meals, and drinks.

If Europe is calling, at least try to balance out the costs by heading east for a while. Parts of Eastern Europe are spectacular but costs can be half what they are in the West. Apart from hotel costs in Prague, nearly everything is a relative bargain in these countries, from food to beer to public transportation. Yet the quality of the "European experience" can still be stunning: great architecture, plenty of cultural entertainment, and outdoor cafés where you can get strong coffee and heavenly pastries.

Turkey, with one foot in Europe and one in Asia, is an even better bargain and has more Roman ruins than Rome. Istanbul is one of the world's great cities: I lived there for five months and never ran out of things to see and do. However, it is just the tip of the iceberg in this attraction-packed country.

For a taste of how different costs can be within Europe, take a look at the chart below.

TYPICAL COSTS IN EUROPEAN CITIES

Oslo	London	Budapest	Istanbul
Meal for Two—simple restaurant			
$16-$24	$10-$20	$4-$8	$3-$10
3-star hotel room, central area			
$100-$155	$85-$170	$35-$65	$35-$80

Sources: Lonely Planet guides, Rough Guides

BEYOND CANCUN AND THE CARIBBEAN

In some ways, Cancun and the Caribbean have become North America's satellite tropical playgrounds. The islands and resorts are set up to please American and Canadian tastes, with prices set at whatever the North Americans will bear. When looking for a "sun and fun" vacation, most people book a trip to this area without even thinking. There's nothing inherently wrong with that; I would be glad to lounge around for a week at nearly any of these places. But I'm usually not willing to pay a month's wages to do so, and there is a huge disparity in price between beaches that are essentially the same.

A few years back, Bermuda's tourism office staffers caught some flak for putting pictures of Florida beaches on one of their brochures. Their defense was, "Most beaches look the same anyway." Having spent a few years traveling around the tropics in many countries, I would have to say they've got a point. In most cases, a beach is a beach is a beach. The differences are often pretty minor: the sand is whiter/browner, the waves are higher/calmer, or there is more/less coral. Unless one of these factors is a huge priority for you, don't hold yourself to a specific location. Be flexible and consider alternative Caribbean locations (Honduras, Panama, or Belize for example) and alternatives to the Caribbean altogether. If you have more time, consider the Caribbean's mirror image in other parts of the world, including the South Pacific and Southeast Asia.

SCUBA DIVING COSTS IN THE CARIBBEAN SEA

Anguilla	Jamaica	Dominican Republic	Honduras (Utilla)
Scuba diving, per day (two dives)			
$85-$105	$60-$80	$50-$75	$20-$60

Sources: Various PADI dive web sites

BEYOND HAWAII

Another location on many Americans' must-see list is Hawaii. It's a U.S. state, so no passport is required, and it is exotic in a safe and packaged kind of way. It's a great place to go golfing or surfing and to see live volcanoes. But is it a deal? Hardly. You can find deals in Hawaii by renting a villa or staying in a small family inn, but most travelers don't go to that much trouble. Plus you still have to pay isolated island prices for food, drinks, gasoline, and everything else that has to be shipped from afar.

If you have solid reasons for going there, such as surf lessons, a sales convention, or volcano hikes, then have a great trip. But if you're traveling that far just to hang out on the beach and drink piña coladas, look at the options for venturing onward to the South Pacific and tropical Asia. You won't find leis and tiki bar glasses, but you may find a better value.

COMPLEMENTARY SUBSTITUTIONS

If you like to drink wine and you read wine articles, you've probably seen some feature at one time comparing very expensive wines with suitable substitutes. The idea is that while you may not be able to afford that perfect $200 Bordeaux for your dinner party, there's probably a reasonably good other option out there for $15-$30 a bottle. A dedicated wine snob *may* notice the difference, but everyone else will taste a very good bottle of wine and enjoy a nice complement to your meal. Television decorating shows dish out the same kind of advice, showing the average family how to get a "$20,000 designer look for $1,000" by substituting similar but less prestigious options.

The same logic can also be applied to parts of the world. One of the main reasons the most expensive Caribbean islands are the most expensive is that they were developed first. Their tourism industry is farther along the growth path, more refined resorts have been built, and the staff costs are higher. They also have more sophisticated and better-funded PR and marketing organizations.

So let's look at Anguilla, home to several resorts that routinely make the "best of" lists in the glossy travel magazines, at rates regularly topping $1,000 per night. These resorts are stunning experiences if you can afford it. If you're Brad Pitt and are looking for seclusion and privacy, they're great. But is the beach really any better in Anguilla than it is in the rest of the Caribbean, including the bargain-priced Dominican Republic? There are thousands of great beaches in the Caribbean, including many postcard-perfect ones on the coast of Mexico and Central America. Almost any of them could serve as a backdrop for one of those enticing Corona beer advertisements.

So is it the food? Is the food better in Anguilla than it is in the Yucatán of Mexico, or Jamaica, or even nearby St. Maarten? Maybe if you're staying at Cap Jaluca, spending a grand or two per night it is, but if you've got that kind of money to blow you're not reading this book. Otherwise, the quality of the beer and seafood are pretty similar throughout the region and the standard thatched-hut restaurant won't look that different from one island to the next. The key difference will come in the form of your dinner bill, which could easily be $50 for two in Anguilla, $30 in Jamaica, $20 in the Dominican Republic, and $10 on the islands off Honduras or Nicaragua.

I'm not picking on Anguilla. I once did an article for *Travel Smart* on finding value-priced hotels on Anguilla; they are out there if you look hard enough. Overall though, the island is just more expensive than many of its neighbors, as are the Virgin Islands and ritzy honeymoon spots you see advertised in bridal magazines, such as St. Kitts and Antigua.

When your choice of destination ends up bringing down the costs, you can follow one of two paths. You can spend less for a similar experience, getting a cheaper vacation and maybe saving enough to take a whole other trip or tacking on more time. Or you can spend the same amount and go up a notch or two in quality and/or quantity. You can afford a suite instead of a room, afford better restaurant meals, or go on more side trips and adventures. If you're at a cheaper destination to start with, the costs for everything you would like to do will be lower. Here are a few ideas for obvious alternatives to pricey destinations.

SAMPLE SUBSTITUTIONS

Standard Destination	Value Substitution
Western Europe	Eastern Europe, Turkey, Quebec City
Top Caribbean Islands	Dominican Republic, Margarita Island, Roatan, Riviera Maya, Belize, Panama
Brazil or Chile	Argentina, Peru, Ecuador, Bolivia
Japan, Hong Kong, Singapore	Nearly anywhere else in Asia
New York, San Francisco, L.A.	Canada or nearly anywhere else in the USA

HOW TO FEEL RICH, WITHOUT ACTUALLY BEING RICH

"How much can prices really vary?" you may be thinking to yourself. Well, here's an example. If you walk into the average bar in Copenhagen, Denmark, how much do you think you'll pay for a draft beer? If you said anything less than $8, you're wrong. Now how much do you think you'll pay if you walk into the average non-tourist bar in Prague and buy a beer? If you said anything over $1.50, you're wrong again. And you'll get a better beer for that $1.50 in Prague than you will for $9 in Copenhagen. Looking at it another way, you could buy a round of the world's best pilsner for yourself and five friends in Prague for what you'd pay for a bottle of Carlsberg in Denmark.

Let's go up a notch and look at meals for two in a restaurant. If you go traveling around the Southeast Asian countries of Thailand, Malaysia, Laos, and Vietnam, you can almost always get a good local meal for a dollar or two. You'll have to go pretty upscale to spend more than $5 per person on lunch. On the other hand, you can easily pay $5 on one apple in Japan and you'll be hard-pressed to even find a bowl of instant ramen noodles for that price at a Tokyo lunch counter. For what it costs to get a sub sandwich and a soda in the U.S., you can get a three-course lunch for two served to you in most of Latin America.

When it comes to hotels, prices between different countries can easily vary by a factor of two or three. For $35, about the price of a Motel 6 in the USA, you'll be lucky to get a private room of any kind in Western Europe, even at a hostel. In much of Latin America, that will get you a nice big hotel room with character, right in the historic center. In the lesser-known areas of Southeast Asia and the Indian subcontinent, it will get you the best room in town, complete with gracious room service, a bellhop to carry your bags, and a nice pool.

At the very top end of the scale, however, these differences can be moot. The average daily wage in Bhutan may be $2 per day, but that doesn't stop Amankora Paro hotel from being able to charge $1,189 per night for a suite. Citizens of the Maldives are quite poor by Western standards, but there are hotels in the Maldives with listed rates of $10,000 per night! If an area is "the place to be" for celebrities and the pampered rich, all bets are off.

COMMON OBJECTIONS

Contrarian travelers get the best deal by going to the places conventional travelers are avoiding. Many people who haven't traveled much, especially Americans, have a natural fear of the unknown. After you've taken a few trips, however, you find that the world is not such a scary place after all.

"I've heard it's dangerous there."

Dangerous compared to what? As an American, I live in a country that leads the developed world in most crime statistics: the most guns, most murders, most armed robberies, most inmates, and most of nearly any other deadly statistic you can think of. The U.S. also has one of the highest traffic fatality rates (partly because we spend so much time in our cars). Yet when Americans think about going overseas, they see the world as being fraught with danger. The Caribbean all-inclusive resorts thrive on this fear. They promise to set you up in a protected enclave, one in which you won't have to interact with any scary locals who are out to rob you.

Look at the facts, however, and you seldom have to worry about anything beyond pickpockets. You are far safer in most cheap destinations than you are in your own hometown. Even Canada, which is perceived as quite safe, still has more reported crime than many cheaper destinations—and at least half of their crimes aren't reported. Statistically, you're more likely to robbed in the U.S. or Canada than you are in Bolivia, Bulgaria, or Vietnam.

Many experienced travelers refer to this perception problem as "The CNN Effect." You'll hear nothing about a country on the news until suddenly something bad happens and it's all the perky newscasters can talk about. A bomb goes off in Casablanca, so everyone stops going anywhere in Morocco. SARS cases are discovered in Toronto, so everyone cancels their trip to Vancouver, even though it's thousands of miles away. Everyone puts off going to India each time Pakistan does some verbal saber rattling in the press. Tourism to Bali dropped after the tsunami hit in Asia, even though it's over a thousand miles away from the affected area. Tourism growth throughout Thailand stagnated for more than a year after the tsunami, even though the disaster hit only a small area on one coast.

Ask most experienced travelers where they wouldn't go because of safety fears and their list will be pretty short. It'll mostly consist of war zones or areas of instability: Colombia, parts of West Africa, Chechnya, Afghanistan, and the like. The occasional political flare-up in a place such as Nepal or Venezuela will naturally inspire some cancelled trips.

You should always do some research on what the situation on the ground is like by checking the "Safety" resources listed at ContrarianTraveler.com and reading international news, but otherwise there is usually far less to worry about than most people think. Our relatives back home seemed to be panicking every few months as my wife and I traveled around the world. What had been blown into a big story in the U.S. was usually run-of-the-mill news where we were, on the scene. Never forget that your chances of dying from cancer are 1 in 499. Your chances of dying from a terrorist hijacking are one in 16,817,784—the latter is about the same as the odds that two dozen coin tosses in a row will come up heads.

"I don't speak the language!"

In the early days of jet travel, language was an issue. Those days are mostly gone: around the world, English rules. Before my first around-the-world journey, I studied Thai language tapes because we were going to spend six weeks in Thailand. Apart from the Thai version of the phrase, "Where is the ____?" I hardly used any of it. It was easier to speak English and look up the rare food words I needed in a phrase book. As we traveled around the world, we often found our tentative questions in the local language answered in English, even in remote villages.

Granted, some basic Spanish will go a long way in Latin America, where their native language is universal enough to make English less necessary. Rural China is a tough place to get around without an English-speaking guide. In most parts of the world, it always helps to learn numbers and at least a few key phrases if you'll be getting out of popular tourist areas. In some African countries, French is more common than English. Otherwise, the world's tourism workers, salespeople, business owners, and students are learning English at a blistering pace. It's the international language of commerce.

Besides, there are also plenty of other ways to communicate: with your body, with drawings, by pointing to things in your phrase book, and even voice inflection. There's a movie called *Ghost Dog* where one character speaks only in English and his best friend speaks only in French. They manage to get by just fine. So will you, once you get used to the notion that every single word doesn't have to be understood for communication to take place.

Travel at Your Own Risk
by Clay Hubbs

In November 1963 my wife and I and our four-year-old son set out from London for India in a seasoned but reasonably fit VW bus. It wasn't a camper but we improvised a bed, crammed the space underneath it with canned goods, and, on the day Kennedy was shot, left for Africa.

We were advised not to. The Automobile Association in the U.K. told us there were no roads across Libya. They were wrong. The State Department in the U.S. said there was a border war between Morocco and Algeria. They were right, but the war did not involve us and the soldiers politely escorted us across the border.

Crossing Libya on a good asphalt road, we saw dozens of burned-out vehicles from the Second World War. We stopped and wandered alone through the incredible ruins of Leptus Magna. We drove up the Red Sea and across to Luxor and down the Nile to Cairo (here there was in fact no road, at least from Luxor to Asyut, but the paths along the irrigation canals were smooth). We did occasionally run into problems, but not the kind predicted by the authorities back in the States. And none that couldn't be solved by relying on the hospitality of the local people. When on the rare occasion it wasn't safe to camp we put up in courtyards, unless our hosts insisted we sleep inside their homes.

In Beirut we met an American couple who had been waiting for six months to cross Syria and Iraq to India, where he had a Fulbright scholarship. They were right to hesitate. The Baath party had just taken power in Baghdad and massacres were occurring. But we had a visa that would soon expire, so we said, "Follow us." The streets of Baghdad were lined with fox-holes and men with machine guns; we were asked to cut our visit short.

The last time we saw our friends we were stuck behind a bus in a snowstorm in the Zagros Mountains. With their four-wheel-drive SUV they managed to go around the trapped bus and on to Tehran. Meanwhile, we holed up in Hamadan, where some USAID people took us in.

And so it went. We returned safe and sound with many stories to tell about Bedouin weddings, narrow escapes from bandits, and visits to places where no unadventurous travelers had ever been. Most of all, our stories were of the people who had befriended us along the way.

Since then, we always read the State Department advisories before we leave for less-traveled destinations. But remembering the advice we received before our first family trip abroad, we weigh the information skeptically.

Dr. Clay Hubbs founded Transitions Abroad *magazine in 1977 to promote travel—real interaction with other cultures—rather than tourism. The "guide to learning, living, and working overseas" promotes cultural understanding and responsible tourism. Hubbs also edits two book series:* Work Abroad: The Complete Guide to Finding a Job Overseas, *and the unique* Alternative Travel Directory.

≈

Destination Questions for the Contrarian Traveler

1. *Do you need to visit a specific place—or are you flexible? Do you just need a beach, or a place to go hiking, or a scuba diving trip?*

2. *Is a certain route on sale? Can you get a cheaper flight and hotel by changing your destination plans?*

3. *Have you considered the overall costs of where you're planning to go, not just the up-front costs such as airfare?*

4. *Is there an easy substitution you can make that will cut your costs by a large amount? The Himalayas or Andes instead of the Alps? Scuba diving in Honduras instead of Australia? A resort in the Dominican Republic, Margarita Island, or in Mexico instead of a resort in Anguilla, Antigua, or Bonaire?*

3

Contrarian Timing

Off Season, Shoulder Season, and "What Are You Doing Here?" Season

The heaviest baggage for a traveler is an empty purse.

—German proverb

Have you ever bought a calendar on January 1? If so, you probably paid half what buyers did a day or two earlier, even though you'll use it the same number of days. Have you ever bought a dozen roses on February 15? Christmas candy on December 26? A bathing suit in September? A leather coat in March? In each case you probably got the goods for half price or less. Same product, same function, but peak season is gone. Smart travelers use this principle to their advantage.

All but the wealthiest travelers will usually find some way to keep their travel budget in line. Even our not-so-savvy Smiths will probably make some attempt now and then to find inexpensive lodging, get a cut-rate airfare, and give some thought to whether they can really afford a particular destination. One often-overlooked variable, however, and one of the most important, is the time of year they visit a particular destination.

The Smiths go to the tropics in January, go skiing in February, and visit national parks in the summer. When they visit New England, they go in autumn, as the leaves are changing.

The Johnsons find alternatives. They know that finding the right time to visit can chop hundreds or thousands of dollars off their travel tab.

HIGH SEASON, HIGH PRICES

In any area that attracts a lot of tourists, high season is expensive. In some cases, downright outrageous. High season can be as long as summer, or as short as New Year's Eve weekend, depending on the location. In any case you are sure to pay top dollar. It costs more to get there, lodging prices shoot up, rental villas get full, and there is almost no room for negotiation. Both crowds and rates are at their maximum. Around Christmas and the New Year's holiday, it's not uncommon to see a flight price jump from $250 to $1,000. A $99 hotel room will suddenly go for $299.

Here are a few examples where your credit card can get maxed out in a hurry:

1. *Europe during the summer school break*

2. *The Caribbean from Christmas through March*

3. *The Canary Islands, Goa, or the Maldives around Christmas break.*

4. *Cancun or Key West during college Spring Break*

5. *Nearly any U.S. or Canadian ski resort on January and February weekends*

6. *Lake resort areas and national parks in the summer*

7. *South American tourist areas during their school break (Jan. and Feb.)*

8. Disney World during any school vacation

9. New England during "leaf-viewing season" in autumn

If you must go to these places at these times, be prepared to open up the wallet. It can be worthwhile to do so for a good reason (see the Epilogue at the end of this book), but finding any kind of a deal can be quite difficult.

Low season is often no picnic, however. Prices are cheap, but they deserve to be. Hurricanes are blowing around the Caribbean and Florida, Egypt feels like the inside of an oven, or clouds obscure the Andes. Coal-heated Turkey and Eastern Europe are pretty dismal in the dead of winter. In parts of Scandanavia and Alaska, you could go for weeks without seeing the sun.

Many beach towns all over the world are literally boarded up in the off-season. It can be a good time to work on a novel or to meditate, but many find the lonely streets and bad weather during low season to be a downer. It depends on the place, however, so do some research. Some spots can be just what the doctor ordered when they're close to empty.

Contrarian travelers match their travel time to the right season, avoiding the absolute worst times to visit an area, whether that means high season and high prices or low season in a place where low season is "What are you doing here?" season.

THE JOY OF SHOULDER SEASON

Shoulder season offers the chance to score a bargain while the getting is still good. This period between high and low season is when prices drop, but the travel experience is still excellent. Rates on everything from lodging to adventure trips usually drop for reasons that are based on demand, not intrinsic value. Europe is still quite nice in the fall, but all the college kids and family vacationers have returned home. The Caribbean and Mexico still have great weather in the late spring, but prices go down because U.S. tourists have stopped thinking about escaping the cold back home. New England is beautiful in the spring, but the crowds are thin because the tree leaves are growing, not changing colors.

Most guidebooks and country-specific web sites have a "when to go" section that describes the ideal time to visit an area, as well as the worst time. In between those two extremes is when you get the best bang for your travel buck. You're not jostling with hundreds of other people to get a room and see the sights, but you're also not arriving when there isn't another soul around and you can't find a place to get dinner.

I've heard people ask, "Oh, how much difference can it really make?" Well, here's how much. In a typical summer, a round-trip flight from Los Angeles to Ireland will run $900 to $1,500 per person in economy coach. In May or September the same route will be on sale for under $500, with a corresponding drop in room rates as a bonus. That fancy Cape Cod inn that starts at $400 per night in the summer? Try $150 per night in September.

In my globetrotting backpacker days, I once rented a nice little guesthouse room with a private bath in Kathmandu, Nepal for $2 per night in early October. When I returned three weeks later from my trek, at the height of the tourist season, the owner wanted $5 for the same room. At the high-end hotels in the same area, nightly rates jumped from $80 to $150 in the space of a few weeks—and then back down again a couple of months later. My arrival flight from India was cheap and half empty. My departure flight was fully booked and 50% more expensive.

It's the same story at the beaches. One hostel room I rented in southern Turkey in September was $5 per night; a month earlier it was $15. Either time you could swim in the water, but I arrived when the tourist season was over. Along the Mayan Riviera coast of the Yucatán in Mexico, I've saved $100 or more per night at an all-inclusive resort by going in May or June, even though nothing has changed except the crowds. A few times I've rented a beach house in the U.S. with friends or another family. When I've done this in July, I've paid absolute top dollar. When I've done it in September, the price has literally dropped in half.

This same scenario plays out all over the world, with the intrinsic laws of supply and demand driving prices up or down. Never forget that airplane seats, beach houses, and hotel rooms are a perishable product: when empty, they generate no revenue. When demand is at its peak, prices will peak as well. When the crowds drop, price changes are necessary to lure a dwindling supply.

THE BEST TIMES FOR SKI BARGAINS

One of the most dramatic disparities can be found at ski resorts. By its nature, this is a business where time is money. Even in the coldest places, the season is limited in length and the natural snow quality can vary from year to year. If people aren't on the slopes when the slopes are open, every business in the area is in trouble. Yet the times most visitors come have little to do with the weather or snowfall—it's all about when they can get off work. So the resorts are half empty during the week, then get jammed on the weekends. You can have the slopes to yourself in early December or in sunny April, but go around a public holiday period in January or February and you'll spend much of your time in lift ticket lines.

This results in some amazing bargains—and a better experience—for anyone who can take some control of when they ski. Locals who live near a ski mountain can get all kinds of mid-week deals on lift tickets. Six resorts in Vermont and New Hampshire share an early-bird-purchase season ticket for $350—with fourteen blackout dates. Buy one good for all days and it jumps to over $600. Anyone who can visit during the week instead of the weekend will also find bargains galore on condo rentals and lodges. Spring skiing is the best deal of all: cheaper packages, warmer weather, and sun.

1. *Last year a 3-day package at Vail (condo lodging and lift ticket) started at $251 per person in April. During President's Weekend holiday the price started at $498 per person.*

2. *Resorts in the Canadian Rockies offer great skiing in the spring at cut-rate prices: a 7-day package with air is frequently less than $800, even from the East Coast.*

3. *Snowfall patterns are different at various resorts. Park City in Utah gets more snow in the first two months of the season than it does in the last four combined. Big Sky in Montana averages ten more inches of snow in March than it gets in January.*

4. *Peak crowds in Europe hit in February and early March. So while January is a crowded time in the U.S., it's not in Europe.*

5. *Watch for deals in newspapers and on the web for early- and late-season deals; often you can get free lessons or a free car rental on top of the lower lodging rates.*

SHOULDER SEASON AROUND THE WORLD

Following are a few specific recommendations for predictable high-value deals around the world, divided by season.

WINTER

While most Americans are obsessed with shopping for presents, travelers can find great values at tropical beaches until Christmas week. Skiers heading to Europe can take advantage of the cheapest flights of the year from the U.S. Bargain rates are available all over Europe, but apart from ski resort areas, stick to southern Europe or do some research on where you are interested.

Flights to Asia generally go down in the winter due to waning demand. In Japan and Korea this can mean experiencing snow-covered temples and cozy rooms with heated floors, while in other parts of Asia it's a tropical paradise. Travelers who want to travel through Southeast Asia in particular should look for the best deal to anywhere in the region and then go overland from there.

Despite this being the summer in South Africa, the best flight prices and package deals are on offer January through April.

Apart from hot areas such as Arizona and Florida, most U.S. and Canadian cities are on sale during the winter. January in Minneapolis may not be much fun, but if you wrap up warm it's not so bad further south. Quebec City and Montreal are enchanting in the winter, for those who have the fortitude to take on the cold.

SPRING

As mentioned before, the ski resorts have a deep base and

sunny days in the spring, but prices for lift tickets and condo rentals take a dive as the country's attention moves away from cold weather sports. This is a quiet time to visit the great American West of the Grand Canyon, Bryce Canyon, and Yellowstone, before the summer vacationers arrive.

Many cruises offer their lowest rates in May, especially "repositioning cruises" that are moving from one part of the world to another. March through May is also a good time for deals in Hawaii, except around school breaks.

Flights to Europe start rising when temperatures do, but rates are still far cheaper than during the summer months. This can be a good time to see the tulip fields of Holland or the green hills of Ireland. Many seasoned travelers consider the spring to be the best time to see Europe, before the hordes arrive.

Starting in mid-April, hotel rates and flights to Mexican beaches and the Caribbean take a drastic drop. From Jamaica to Tulum to Barbados, the water is warm and the beaches are less crowded. Flights to Central and South America often drop in tandem—except around Carnival and Easter.

The northern hemisphere's spring is autumn in Australia, New Zealand, and South Africa, with shoulder season rates on flights and lodging. March through May are great months to visit hot and dry countries such as Morocco, Egypt, or Jordan.

SUMMER

Summer is the toughest time to find a bargain, mostly because demand is so high from North Americans, Europeans, and the Japanese. Add June weddings and honeymoons to the mix and there are a lot of people on the move.

However, in June and early July, Caribbean and Mexican destinations are at their lowest shoulder season prices, before Europeans start filling resorts in August and rains start picking up. For budget travelers, less touristed destinations provide the best lodging and diving deals: Venezuela's Margarita Island, the Bay Islands of Honduras, or the islands scattered off the coasts of Belize, Panama, and Nicaragua.

June to September is shoulder season in Kenya and Tanzania, when the high season is over, but the weather is still cool and dry. This is an excellent time to go on a safari.

In Canada, there is a short shoulder season for national parks in the first two weeks of June and the last two weeks of August.

While it is summer in North America, it is winter in the southern hemisphere, but you will find beach weather without the summer humidity in Rio de Janeiro or Bahia. Few Brazilians are on the move during this time, so rooms are plentiful.

If you can stand the heat, you will find flights and hotels only slightly higher than the spring in Southeast Asia, including Hong Kong, Thailand, and Vietnam. Meanwhile, in the U.S., prices in hot areas fall where the heat rises the most. Count on lower flights and room rates in cities such as Miami, New Orleans, Phoenix, and Las Vegas.

FALL

September is still swimming weather in the mid-Atlantic, with much warmer water than June on many Atlantic beaches. House or condo rentals on the coasts of the Carolinas or California can be half what they are in the summer. In the southern Atlantic, however, it is important to keep an eye on the hurricane forecast.

Due to the end of school breaks, U.S. attractions are far less busy after Labor Day weekend, apart from Thanksgiving and Christmas. National Parks are less crowded and you can find better deals on nearby lodging. This can also be a time of great weather in the hot, dry areas in the west or south.

Flights to Europe usually start going on sale in October. Lodging rates drop in tandem, even at some hostels, and with a wider selection of rooms it is easier to be choosy. In southern European cities, the weather can still be mild until mid-November or early December.

The summer cruise ship crowds have mostly left the Greek Islands and Turkey, but the early fall weather is still sunny, the party kids have gone home, and hotels are open to bargaining. It is already getting cold in Alaska at this time, but the waning Alaskan cruises in September offer crisp views and bargain rates.

Mid-October to mid-December marks the transition from the wet season to dry season in Costa Rica and Panama: lush jungle trips before the big crowds arrive.

While August through November is hurricane season in the Caribbean, the southern Caribbean islands are nearly always out of harm's way. This means you can generally travel to Aruba, Bonaire, Curacao, Margarita Island, and Trinidad and Tobago at reduced prices, without much risk of high winds.

Against the Tide in the Off Season
by Max Hartshorne

My parents took us to Atlantic City in February, 1973. In those days, Donald Trump had not yet arrived, and the ritziest place on the boardwalk was the ancient Chalfont Hadden Hall hotel, a towering edifice that would later be torn down to make way for Harrah's Casino. Atlantic City had yet to become the gambling mecca of the Jersey Shore.

I wasn't sure why my parents wanted to take us. After some grueling summer afternoons with us fighting like like cats and dogs in the hot car on the way up to Cape Cod, I was sure we had taken our last family trip. But as we headed down the New Jersey Turnpike for that paradise by the sea, I realized it was their idea of a romantic weekend. So they got us kids a room and they had their own across the hall.

February in Atlantic City is bleak. Winds blow across the boardwalk swirling trash, and the winter ocean is fiercely uninviting. But inside our two rooms in this magnificent hotel, we were at peace. Room service brought asparagus with hollandaise sauce and thick steaks, and we watched our favorite Saturday night TV shows while our parents "reconnected" across the hall. The price was right, and that made this grand hotel affordable, even with two rooms.

Why go to Atlantic City in February? Or St.Croix in July? As a friend told me who often visits the Caribbean in the sultry summer months, "the temperature is the same in the winter or the summer....it's just that nobody goes in July."

Many people love going to Martha's Vineyard and Nantucket, but they usually choose July or August to descend upon these little islands, joining the hordes trying to park huge SUVs in small cobblestone spaces, or negotiating the narrow streets by moped. But these summer islands are perfect examples of why traveling off season is so much more rewarding. In late September the water is finally warm enough to plunge into without fearing a heart attack or watching your manhood disappear up inside you. The light of September is clearer and brighter without the haze of the summer.

Casting out a line on a beach anywhere in Massachusetts in October is also more likely to get you a fish. So the next time you are making travel plans, think beyond the norm. Stretch a bit, and consider that if you have a choice between seeing and being seen or actually getting to enjoy the loveliness of the place you are visiting, you'll probably enjoy the latter and be glad you went against the tide, during the off season.

Max Hartshorne is editor of GoNomad.com, a comprehensive resource center that provides inspiration and information for independent and alternative travelers.

Timing Questions for the Contrarian Traveler

1. *Is there a really good, valid reason you are traveling to a peak destination during high season?*

2. *Are you limited as to when you can go on vacation? If so, and it coincides with holidays, can you visit an international destination that is on a different schedule? Or an area that doesn't get deluged with tourists?*

3. *Can you make adjustments to your schedule to avoid peak season?*

4. *Have you thought about going a different direction than everyone else—such as going to the tropics in May or June, or skiing in South America when it's our summer?*

4

CONTRARIAN FLIGHTS
Market Forces and Those
Who Ride Them

"Air transport is just a glorified bus operation."
—Michael O'Leary, CEO of Ryanair

Ten or fifteen years ago, this would have been the longest and most important chapter in the book. Back then, dozens of books per year used to be solely devoted to getting a better deal on airfare. Some talked extensively about options that have mostly disappeared, such as courier flights. But ever since the internet really took hold and pricing became more transparent, it hasn't taken a lot of sleuthing to score a reasonable airfare deal.

With excess competition, flights are cheaper now than they have ever been, even for business travelers with no flexibility. Adjusted for inflation, U.S. airfares have fallen 50% since 1978. With the oldest airlines on a first-name basis with bankruptcy judges, some say this can't last. In my opinion, as long as Southwest, Ryanair, and EasyJet are making a profit, low prices are here to stay.

Obsessing over the price of a flight used to make sense. On a typical far-flung vacation, the airfare could make up half the expense. Now it's more likely to be a small fraction of the total. This is especially true within the U.S. or within Europe. Asia is coming on strong with its own group of cut-rate budget carriers.

Finding a good deal on a flight now mostly comes down to three actions: keeping tabs on prices, timing your trip correctly, and accumulating frequent-flyer miles correctly.

Comfort, however, seems to have gone out through the cabin ventilation ducts. What were once called "full service" airlines (now more accurately called "legacy airlines") have done a terrible job of creating any kind of brand identity or service differentiation, especially for coach passengers. Instead they have tried to go head-to-head with the budget airlines and have made themselves a commodity in the process. They keep cutting services in order to compete. After taking away meals, pretzels, magazines, and pillows—or trying to charge extra for them—most of the hub-and-spoke airlines now offer fewer frills than their budget rivals. Some are even charging a fee for curbside check-in. It's the perfect Harvard Business School case study for bad business strategy. Of course we also have ourselves as consumers to blame. All things being equal in the schedule, we pick the cheapest flight nearly every time. Now we're getting what we've paid for.

Still, there are ways for the contrarian traveler to get an edge in this environment. Once again, it's just a matter of not doing what the masses are doing. With a few simple adjustments, you can make the most of an experience that for many people has become far from pleasant. If you do a better job of pooling your frequent-flyer mileage, you can even move to the front cabin now and then.

This chapter will look at strategies for obtaining the best flight value. It will discuss how to make the most of frequent-flyer programs instead of using them haphazardly like most leisure travelers do. It will also go over adjustments to be made for domestic and international flights, with some strategies for getting at least a modicum of comfort along the way.

THE AIRLINE BUSINESS

You don't have to be a business news junkie to see that most airlines are in trouble. When I started writing this book, fully half the U.S. airline seats were being operated by airlines in bankruptcy. Many storied international ones, such as British Airways, Alitalia, Air France, and Cathay Pacific, would also be in bankruptcy if it weren't for some kind of government bailout. SwissAir wasn't so lucky and is gone.

Airlines need your business badly. As you've probably noticed, they don't act like it. Airlines need dedicated, intelligent employees. As you've also probably noticed, they're not doing much to hold onto this kind of employee. We've entered an ironic age where the "budget" airlines, such as Southwest and JetBlue, offer better service and amenities for the majority of passengers than the legacy airlines do. The only people getting more from the legacy airlines are those in business class or first class.

There are a lot of reasons we are in this situation. Your average high school student is probably better at managing his finances than the average airline executive. The airlines spent lavishly during the good times and then had nothing to invest during the bad. And "the bad" got really bad after the 9/11 attacks and then the rise in fuel prices. The hub-and-spoke system's faults became obvious when more nimble airlines started offering far more direct flights. As I said before, we have also collectively sped up the decline of the legacy airlines by making a rock bottom price our first priority when booking.

What does it all mean? It means old assumptions are often wrong. You need to leverage your e-mail inbox to get the best deals and then still shop around. Loyalty pays, but hedge your bets. You need to learn the quirks of your favored airline(s). Mostly, you need to watch what the masses are doing and then adjust to avoid the crowds.

OLD ASSUMPTIONS, BAD ASSUMPTIONS

A lot of things that were drilled into travelers' heads over the years are no longer true. Contrarian travelers continually question conventional wisdom.

"Book in advance to get the best deals." This used to be true, with fourteen days being the magic number, but it is only sometimes true now. Last-minute deals trump advance ones unless a plane is full. Plus different airlines follow different strategies for pricing, so you need to follow yours for a while to find the right window.

"Stay over a Saturday to get the best rate." Again, this used to be true, but usually isn't anymore. We can thank Southwest's policy (copied by most other budget airlines) of pricing each segment independently. As a result, airlines have mostly given up on penalizing business travelers—the whole reason for the Saturday-stay rule.

"A Eurail Pass is the best value for travel in Europe." Budget airlines have turned the European travel experience upside down. Trains are a more pleasant way to travel, but flights on dozens of budget flyers such as Ryanair, EasyJet, or Berlin Air are often cheaper. To figure out which airlines serve a particular route, check WhichBudget.com or others listed in the resources.

"U.S. carrier flights are as good or better than foreign carriers for international trips." This probably hasn't been true for twenty years, but many U.S. and Canadian flyers still root for the home team when traveling abroad. In reality, foreign carriers offer a better experience in coach and a lot better experience at the front of the cabin. Discount consolidator 1stAir conducted a survey of frequent international flyers on the subject. Over 80% agreed with the statement that "domestic carriers operating international routes continue to post losses because their premium-class products are not at the same standards as their foreign flag competitors." If you are using mileage for a trip then fine, fly on a domestic carrier to get the benefits. Otherwise, you'll probably have a better flight on a foreign carrier—and in some cases you can use your domestic airline's mileage with one of their foreign partners.

PROPERLY USING THE WEB AND E-MAIL

Our sample couple the Smiths get a decent deal on airfare when they travel, so we can forgive them for not spending a lot of time on research. As long as they use one of the travel aggregators (such as Kayak or Sidestep) and check the appropriate budget airline sites for their route, they will do O.K. The only people who are vastly overpaying in this environment are the ones who have to go on very short notice on a crowded plane or those who are flying to a popular destination during a peak period (See Chapter 3). Still, with prices fluctuating so much from week to week, the Smiths often have a nagging feeling they could have done better.

The Johnsons never have that feeling. They know they are always getting the best value out there. Our contrarian travelers don't go find the best deals. They let the best deals come to them. On a regular basis, they receive five key newsletters in their e-mail inbox:

1. SmarterTravel.com's rundown of sale flights from the Johnson's home airport.

2. Travelocity's Fare Watcher alert for routes they regularly fly

3. A special deals newsletter from their #1 preferred airline

4. A special deals newsletter from their #2 preferred airline

5. A newsletter with limited-time offers from a clearing-house such as TravelZoo or Sherman's Travel

These specific providers could change and others could take their place. Anyone living outside the U.S. will need to find country-specific matches that serve the same purpose. The overall strategy is to make sure you are receiving the best deals on a regular basis. That way you don't have to waste time surfing a bunch of random comparison sites to find them.

A service like SmarterTravel's will ensure that you know what opportunities are out there from your own airport. You may not be searching for a cheap deal to Vancouver this month, but if one pops up for $129 per person, maybe that's where you should be headed. You may have been planning a trip from London to Bermuda. But if a flight from London to Barbados goes on sale for $199, a change of plans would make a lot of sense.

Travelocity's fare watcher is an amazing thing. You set a price level for when you want to be alerted, then just go about your business. When a flight price breaks below that threshold, you get an e-mail alert. If it doesn't, you don't. You can set up to five combinations of cities and be vigilent without even trying.

Just remember that some airlines don't share information with these booking sites. Which means another step. For whatever airlines you use the most, you should be on their e-mail list. For many of the budget airlines, such as Southwest, you need to subscribe to their own list to see their weekly deals. If you don't have one or two preferred airlines, you should. More on that in the frequent-flyer section later. It never hurts to do a price check with a "meta search engine" to be sure you didn't miss anything: see web sites such as Kayak, Sidestep, and Mobissimo.

Finally, you should be on the list for a service such as TravelZoo or Sherman's Travel, where fantastic values on flights, hotels, and packages are posted on a weekly basis. There are other sites in a variety of countries that specialize in similar local deals. Whatever your preference, these e-mail newsletters can save you a fortune—and won't cost you a dime to subscribe. See ContrarianTraveler.com for continually updated links.

IT'S WORTH IT TO BE LOYAL—SORT OF

In his book, *I'm a Stranger Here Myself*, Bill Bryson says, "I must fly 100,000 miles a year, yet I have accumulated only 212 air miles divided among twenty-three airlines." This is funny, but it's not far off the mark for many people. When the Smiths book a flight, they choose the cheapest flight that fits their time frame, regardless of the airline. They belong to a half-dozen frequent-flyer programs, with a smattering of miles in each one. When they have a complaint or need a favor, they have trouble getting anyone to listen. They always fly in coach and always will.

The Johnsons book most of their flights on one of two airlines: a legacy airline and a budget airline. When they can't book their flight on one of these two, they try to choose a partner airline that will still earn them usable frequent-flyer points. They only choose an alternate if it is going to save them a significant sum. When they have a complaint or need a favor from their airline, they are treated like the loyal customers they are. If they are traveling a lot in one year, they can reach elite status, enabling them to get more perks for the whole next calendar year.

Loyalty Pays
by Joel L. Widzer

The idea of getting the best value for your travel dollars is the core of my travel philosophy. I do this by building mutually beneficial relationships with quality travel providers.

The mutually beneficial relationship theory works because it provides customers with the best value for their travel dollar, while the travel provider attracts repeat business by offering "the right customers" preferred services.

The more than 2.5 million miles I have accumulated with Delta Air Lines has served me well. My loyalty has granted me access to a bevy of benefits including:

- First-class check-in, early boarding, priority seating, and priority waitlists

- Entrée to the faster frequent-traveler security lines

- Complimentary upgrades to business class or first class

- Bonus miles on flights, ranging from 25% to 200%

- Easier redemption of frequent-flyer awards

- Free airport lounge privileges.

The good news is that you don't need to fly millions of miles to receive these types of preferred services. To gain distance from the crowd, you need as few as 25,000 miles in one year. If that seems like a lot, watch your preferred airlines for special deals. My sixteen-year-old daughter achieved elite status with Delta by taking one flight out of Syracuse, New York, during a special promotion. She received complimentary upgrades on her next four flights.

The key is choosing the right travel provider.

Choosing the right travel provider depends on your perception of the provider's quality, service, price, and the degree of importance you attach to these factors. While every traveler has his or her individual preferences and needs, it is fair to say that all travelers want quality service, convenience, and comfort—at a fair price.

When you see a company as the right travel provider, the more likely you are to give them your repeat business. When a travel provider sees *you* as the right or loyal customer, the more likely you are to receive preferential treatment for giving that travel provider your loyalty, and thus an economic advantage over its competitors.

Loyalty can also save you in a pinch. I once made the mistake of making a reservation at the Hilton in San Francisco for the wrong date. When I called the hotel a week before my intended arrival they told me that my reservation was for a few weeks past. Wanting to reward my past loyalty to the Hilton brand, the hotel's agent reversed the no-show charges and honored the original rate, which was $100 lower than the current rate.

Whether you reach first-tier elite status, or ultra status, continued loyalty is the consumer's half of the equation, rewarded with upgrades, preferential service, and the occasional special reward.

The key to a good relationship is continuity. In real life, becoming seduced by every temptress that comes along would result in utter chaos. In my opinion, this is the same thing as chasing the absolute lowest fare or the latest loyalty fad.

Oh, and one more thing. If your airline or travel partner fails, the one thing guaranteed to transfer to another airline is your elite membership. In fact, if you decide to change carriers mid-year, most airlines will match your level of elite membership.

Joel Widzer is the author of The Penny Pincher's Passport to Luxury Travel, *now in its second edition. Widzer is a sought-after speaker who appears frequently in the media. He holds a doctoral degree in the field of industrial organizational psychology and is the managing partner of JlwConsulting.*

By aligning themselves with just one or two airlines, the contrarian travelers learn what business traveler road warriors already know: loyalty results in benefits. The ultimate prize, of course, is elite status in a frequent-flyer program of a legacy airline. As Joel Widzer mentions in "Loyalty Pays," those who reach this level are able to board first, frequently upgrade to first class, and get lots of other perks. At least 25,000 actual miles flown in a calendar year is generally the entry point. Most people who only travel for pleasure won't reach that level without taking several international flights in the course of a year (or one really long one), but special promotions can tip the scale more in the leisure traveler's favor.

There are other perks to being loyal, however. Flight miles add up a lot faster when they are concentrated in one or two programs. Airlines are constantly running bonus programs for booking direct, for checking in online, or for signing up for their newsletter. Regular flyers get offers in the mail for companion flight deals, unadvertised discounts, or discounted airport club admissions. Plus let's face it, if you are a harried check-in counter clerk dealing with a handful of demanding customers, are you going to help out the one who flies on your airline once every five years, or the one who has flown with you five times in one year?

I don't believe any legacy airline deserves all my business, however. On many routes from my own mid-sized city, I can fly on a budget airline for half the price, in half the time, on a larger plane, and get service that's twice as friendly. When it's a choice between two tiny commuter jets through an out-of-the-way hub, or a direct flight on a plane where you can actually stand up in the aisle—for less money—loyalty only goes so far. So it also pays to build loyalty with a budget airline. You won't ever get first-class perks, but most make it easy to get and use a free flight, which is worth real money.

BUILD UP MILEAGE—BOTH ON AND OFF THE GROUND

One penny.

That's about what a frequent-flyer mile is worth. If you cash in your miles for international flights or perpetually expensive business- or first-class routes, you can get that worth up to as much as four cents, but a penny is the norm for most people. For example, 25,000 miles will get you a $250 gift certificate to a retailer in many programs, or get you on a domestic flight that probably wouldn't cost you more than $250.

With that in mind, it doesn't make much sense to pay $85 per year for a credit card just to earn one mile per dollar. You would have to charge over $8,500 in one year just to break even, assuming you don't pay a cent of interest. If the credit card offer comes with 15,000 bonus miles and a 5% discount on all tickets, as my preferred airline's card did, that's a different story. I came out ahead after spending my first dollar: $150 worth of miles for $85, plus a guaranteed discount on tickets I was going to buy anyway. For your situation, you need to use your spending history and a calculator to figure it all out.

My American Express card has delivered a lot of perks. It costs me close to a hundred bucks a year, but its Membership Miles program pays plenty of dividends. I charge half of what I spend each month on there (including many regular household bills), so I build up a lot of miles. I can then transfer those miles to any of several airline programs to top off the mileage I have in there. So if I'm 4,000 short of a free flight to South America, as I was recently, I can transfer just those 4,000 and I'm on my way. Plus the program regularly runs bonus programs: transfer 10,000 miles, for example, and get 2,000 extra miles added on top. Free mileage without leaving the computer chair. (Diner's Club runs a similar program.) An uncle of mine charged his daughter's university tuition on his mileage card each semester. Well before she graduated, they had enough to take the whole family to Hawaii!

The AmEx program and individual airline ones also maintain "mileage malls." You go onto the airline's site, log in, and then go shopping at one of dozens of online retailers. You get at least one mile for every dollar you spend, more often two or three miles per dollar. This is a great example of no cost mileage. You were going to buy those books or electronic gadgets anyway, right? So get something out of the deal! Make the payment with a mileage-earning card and you'll get more miles again on top of it. After a year of doing this by habit and concentrating your flights with one or two airlines, you'll be paying nothing for your next flight—or kicking back with more space after an upgrade to business class.

If all this point-watching and scheming seems unimportant or too much trouble, keep in mind what Ron Lieber pointed out in a *Wall Street Journal* story: "By not participating, you're subsidizing the rewards of all of us who know how to game the system successfully."

Learn How Your Airlines Operate

Different airlines follow different pricing strategies. You can't bank on getting the best fare until you know how your preferred ones operate.

- Southwest publishes every fare option transparently in the open. When a flight looks like it's too empty, they drop the price in their weekly sale alert.

- EasyJet runs ridiculously cheap intro fares to kick off a new route. After they reach critical mass, the price settles at a fairly predictable rate until capacity drops and a sale kicks in.

- Delta prices often start off low for periods far in advance and rise as time goes on, up to a capped rate. At the last minute, poor-selling segments go on sale.

- Continental starts its advance purchase prices unusually high (often higher than Delta's capped maximum), then steps them down as time goes by or a competitor runs a sale. In the last week, unsold seats often drop below budget airline rates.

Four more airlines would present four slightly different strategies. As you can see, there's no overall trend, except that the gamble of waiting until a day or two before departure can pay off big across the board. Buying tickets months in advance on Delta may be smart. On Continental it's dumb unless it's a holiday and you can't afford to take chances. On Southwest it probably doesn't matter much either way.

The last-minute option is a good bet for the flexible. By taking advantage of this, I've flown round trip to international destinations for less than $200 and domestic ones for less than $80—taxes included. This won't work, however, if you have a 10:00 A.M. meeting on Tuesday with your most important client. Or if your family of four is trying to get to Disney World and you have hotel reservations already. Or it's a Thanksgiving holiday. In those cases, figure out how your favored airlines work so you can pursue the right strategy in advance.

THE ADVANTAGE OF PACKAGES

I wear my biases quite openly, and one is that I am not a big fan of standard package tours. When a hundred people fly together, stay together, go on excursions together, and fly home together, that's not going to be much of a travel experience. It's a guided high school field trip taken by adults.

Having said that, if your only goal is to get away from work and go hang out on a beach for a week or less, package deals can have a definite cost advantage. It annoys independent travelers to no end, but an air/hotel package deal is often far cheaper than booking the two separately. Sometimes the discount is so great that the whole package is cheaper than a flight booked by itself. Or a rental car may be thrown in for free. In these cases, it makes sense to just buy the package deal, assuming the dates line up, even if you don't want to stay in that hotel the whole time. Throw away a few hotel nights and explore—the room didn't really cost you much anyway.

Also, many of these companies sell unfilled seats on their charter flights. If it's a slow time of year, these can be far cheaper than a regular carrier seat. See the resources site for links to Apple Vacations, Vacation Express, SunTrips, and others. You can find similar examples in any country where a lot of people take international group trips, such as England, Germany, Australia and Japan.

A group fare isn't always cheaper though, so you have to keep a calculator by your computer keyboard. A bit of unsavory news came out of the US Airways/America West merger: it turns out that America West had been rewarding travel agents with incentives if they charged *groups* more than what the tickets would cost individually. As this book went to press, US Airways was planning to adopt the policy company-wide. So much for volume discounts.

LOOK BEYOND THE OBVIOUS

London-based company Skytraxx surveyed more than 12 million travelers in 94 countries in a customer satisfaction poll. In no surprise to American frequent flyers, not one U.S. airline placed in the top ten. (Southwest and JetBlue fared the best.) The top three were Cathay Pacific, Qantas, and Emirates.

A story in *The Wall Street Journal* found that smaller, lesser-known international carriers such as EVA and Lan Chile consistently delivered better prices, more amenities, and better service. My best coach flight ever was on Malaysia Airlines. My business class flight on South African Airways was heavenly. Anyone who has flown Singapore Airlines has trouble going back to the inferior domestic airlines. These days, bigger isn't better. Throughout Asia, a dozen airlines you have never heard of are making it easy to get from point A to point B for $100 or less. Check out Tiger Airways, Oasis Hong Kong, Nok Air, AirAsia, and the others that will have popped up after this book was written. The specific names are not what you need to remember. The point is that there are a lot of options out there that you won't find on Orbitz or Expedia. Go to country-specific travel portals and guidebooks to find out about local deals.

For international flights, do some nosing around before booking. Sometimes you can find consolidators who resell tickets on specific routes on the cheap. (Chicago to Warsaw, New York to Jamaica, San Francisco to China.) Check ads in the Sunday paper or in local papers catering to immigrants. Also, note that some international airlines are positioning themselves as budget options, with capped prices. If you are going to Europe, for example, look into Aer Lingus or IcelandAir. For the Caribbean and Mexico, check Frontier, ATA, or Spirit. A few upstarts are even offering business-class-only flights across the Atlantic. More money than flying coach, of course, but lots of comfort at a lower price than on most legacy carriers.

HALFWAY AROUND THE WORLD? KEEP ON GOING!

If you are flying to a far-flung destination and you have some time to see other places, keep going! You can buy a round-the-world (RTW) ticket from an alliance of airline partners or put one together with an agency that specializes in this. If you are flying to India or Africa, for example, you could then stop in Bangkok, Hong Kong, Sydney, and Hawaii before coming home. Or any other dream spots that are on the way.

With the major airlines, there are three partnerships that can put a trip together: One World, Star Alliance, and SkyTeam. This is the best option if you want to collect all the mileage and fly on familiar airlines—or if you are an elite-level member who wants the royal treatment during the entire trip.

If you are on a budget or are more adventurous, work out an itinerary with an agency such as STA, Air Brokers, or AirTreks. You may fly on some airlines you have never heard of, but the price is right and you have more options since you are not limited to a certain set of partners. These can be as little as $1,300 with five stops.

Round-the-world tickets are an especially good deal in business class, where the difference between a round-trip ticket to a faraway place and one that keeps going is minimal. Road warriors with fat frequent-flyer mileage accounts can even purchase a RTW ticket with mileage.

LEGROOM AND SEATS FROM HELL

The airline industry may be in trouble, but it's not because of a lack of flyers. Airline traffic has recovered from the last slump, and is growing at 15% to 20% around the globe. This means the empty planes of a few years ago are history. Flights are jammed and so are seats. Despite all the bankruptcy news, U.S. airlines actually filled close to 80% of their domestic seats in 2005, meaning your chances of being on a half-full airplane then were very slim.

This trend looks set to continue. Airlines have squeezed more seats onto their planes and legroom has decreased—while the odds of sitting next to an obese flyer have increased with our collective waistlines and hips. So what do you do?

Here are the easy answers. Implementing them is the challenge:

1. Fly business class or first class.

2. Pick a bulkhead or exit row seat for more legroom.

3. Fly on an Asian or Middle Eastern carrier for more legroom when going abroad.

4. Fly at unpopular times to have a better chance of avoiding a middle seat.

None of these are ever a given. Flying business or first class usually requires a lot of money, elite status, a lot of frequent-flyer miles, or all of the above. Don't rule it out, however. These seats are sometimes sold cheaper than you would expect and several consolidators specialize in steeply discounted business- and first-class rates.

Everyone wants an exit row seat, including the poor tall guys stuck in coach on the flight, so you have to arrive very early or be good at sweet-talking the check-in person. Bulkhead seats offer more room, but they're also favored by moms and dads flying with lap kids, so look out.

Flying on a foreign airline is great when you can do it; Singapore Airlines offers a full six inches more of legroom than United or Delta. On domestic and inter-European flights, there's no way out: they're all equally cramped in standard coach.

The "least-crowded flight" option offers the most control. The busiest times for business travelers are the first flight or two each weekday morning (especially on Mondays) and the afternoon to early evening flights on Fridays. Friday nights, Saturday morning, and Sunday afternoon and evening are popular with leisure travelers. So the ideal time to fly is midday during the week or Saturday afternoon if you can swing it. If you want to see when the peak airport times are, the

U.S. Transportation Security Agency (www.tsa.gov) publishes average security line wait times throughout the day at each U.S. airport. Some experts predict that international flights are going to be less crowded than domestic flights in the coming years because of added capacity there and cut capacity at home. So you may find a better deal and more room flying to Stockholm than you will flying to Seattle.

One site worth bookmarking is SeatGuru.com. If you know the airline and type of plane, it will show you the configuration of seats so you can stay away from the bathroom, or seats that don't lean back, or a middle seat. Some airline's booking sites also let you see what is available before you book. Take advantage of these and try to pick out your seats upon booking. Don't leave it to chance when arriving at the gate. Even on budget airlines, you can increase your odds of a good seat by checking in online ahead of time, putting you in the earliest group to board.

Flight Questions for the Contrarian Traveler

1. Are you basing your flight decisions on assumptions that have gone out of date?

2. Are you flying on one or two airlines for the bulk of your flights to build up mileage, or just automatically taking the cheapest one? Are you adding miles with every single credit card and online purchase?

3. If looking for a rock-bottom international deal, have you tried consolidators, charter airlines, or airlines not listed on the main booking sites?

4. Are you taking steps each flight to make sure you don't get stuck in one of the worst seats on the plane, or are you just taking your chances?

5

Contrarian Lodging

Do You Really Need Turndown Service in Fiji?

> *"There are, after all, only so many things one can say about sumptuous meals, luxury transportation, jade-green golf courses, and expensive rooms in five-star hotels."*
>
> —Robert Strauss, "Confessions of a Travel Writer"

This chapter is about widening your horizons when it comes to lodging. To start it off, I'm going to tell a typical tale of one city's hotel options.

I have a modest little beach house on the Gulf Coast of Mexico, near the lovely colonial city of Mérida. Usually when my family flies in, we spend a night or two in Mérida itself. When most Americans visit Mérida, they stay at one of two places: the Hyatt or the Fiesta Americana. The first choice is the best-known international chain hotel. The second is the fanciest overall hotel. If I were to spend the night in either place with my wife and daughter, it would cost me anywhere from $90 to $170 a night before taxes. Not a bad deal in international terms, but we'd be sharing a conventional hotel room, with furnishings not much different than we see at any U.S. hotel. The public areas are mostly decorated in that typical bland international style you see all over the world. We would be a full thirteen blocks from the historic center, which is too far to walk. Most of the restaurants in the area cater to foreigners or those who want to act like foreigners.

Instead, we stay at a funky little hotel called Luz en Yucatán, housed in a historic colonial mansion. We get a spacious suite with a kitchenette. The place oozes character: the public areas are full of local artifacts and antiques. Tropical plants encircle the picturesque courtyard swimming pool. We are next to a park that often hosts live music shows and are three short blocks from the city's historic grand plaza. Dozens of interesting restaurants are a five-minute walk away. The rate? From $40 to $80 depending on which suite, since every one is different.

The Smiths would never hear about the likes of Luz en Yucatán, much less stay there. They wouldn't stay at one of the dozen other great little independent hotels in the area either. When the Smiths go on vacation, they stay at a nice, predictable chain hotel, with a name they recognize. There are no great surprises, but few bad ones either. Their room looks similar to the ones they have stayed at in other cities, except for a few pieces of localized artwork hanging on the wall now and then. The price is also predictable—similar to what they would pay in any U.S. city, maybe a bit more or less now and then. They can find the brand of liquor they like to drink at home in the hotel bar. The buffet table and menu won't have anything too weird and unrecognizable. Most of the people they talk to speak English since most of the guests are similar to the Smiths. They don't meet many other guests anyway: privacy is highly valued.

When the Johnsons go on vacation, sometimes they rent a villa or do a home exchange. If they do stay at a hotel, they stay at an interesting property with a strong sense of place. Sometimes the setting and amenities are just fair, sometimes they are fantastic. Occasionally the service is slow and sometimes the desk clerk doesn't speak fluent English. But the price is far less than in an international chain hotel, often a fraction of what a similar hotel room would cost at home. Usually the property is locally owned, so many times the Johnsons meet the owners and get personalized attention. The location is usually convenient for walking and taking public transportation.

No two places they have stayed have been the same. Often they can tell where they are the minute they enter their room. If there is a bar, the selection will vary from a fridge of beer and juice to a full bar, but local brews or wines will always be on tap. The restaurant, if there is one, will feature food that is grown in the region, so local dishes will be prominent. The guests are from various countries and speak a variety of languages. The Johnsons know because they have met many of them in the communal lounge.

In the book *A Sense of Place*, author Michael Shapiro interviews guidebook legend Arthur Frommer. "I have stayed at every kind of deluxe facility imaginable," Frommer says. "I regard them as one more crushing bore after the next."

I too have stayed in a lot of opulent hotels, both on my dime and on someone else's. Some have been truly fantastic, while most have quickly faded from memory. Much of the time my wife has been with me. She enjoys a good pampering as much as anyone. But she is also very social. After a few days in a deluxe hotel, she starts getting cranky, especially if I'm out doing research all day in town or am at a conference. The problem is that she doesn't meet many people in these luxury places—they're not set up for that. When she does manage to start a conversation, she complains that the people often want to talk about work and home rather than what's going on outside the hotel walls. She's ready to move on to a less sterile setting, where the sounds of conversation and laughter are louder than subdued classical music and silver clinking on fine china plates.

I also have to mention one of my biggest pet peeves: the more expensive the hotel, the more you will pay for "incidental charges." That free wi-fi internet access at Comfort Inn and Holiday Inn Express? Try $10 per day and up at the Sheraton or InterContinental. Those free local calls at the Motel 6 or the corner hostel? Try $2 per call at the W Hotel. Want to get your laundry done? The little guesthouse in Chiang Mai will send it out to a service for you and take a modest cut. The luxury palace down the street will charge you the price of a new outfit. Many expensive hotels nickel and dime you to death with charges to use the gym, charges for a newspaper, "energy surcharges," fees to restock the overpriced minibar, and even "resort fees" for facilities that should be a part of the room rate.

Inflated add-on fees are big business. PriceWaterhouse-Coopers estimates that these extra charges add $100 million in annual revenue to the big hotel chains' bottom lines. There's a rumor that cell phone reception is bad in some big hotels by design: they use a device that thwarts reception so that guests will be forced to use the hotel's phone system. The Microtel chain, on the other hand, lets you call anywhere in the continental U.S. for free, so they couldn't care less if your cell phone reception is perfect.

Break Out of the Cocoon
by Rob Sangster

I love luxury hotels, at least the ones that are oases of art and paragons of pampering. I've stayed in a fair number of them but, much more often, I just go out of my way to visit them for high tea or an evening cocktail. I certainly understand why those for whom money has no meaning are addicted to the finest luxury hotels.

A much larger number of travelers routinely choose international chain hotels. I understand that, too: easy to reserve and very predictable. In fact, many of these chains are at their best overseas.

On balance though, many luxury hotels and nearly all chain hotels are uninspiring clones that rob travelers of some of the essence of the experience they've come so far to enjoy. These places appeal to English-speaking guests who, oddly, don't tend to talk much with one another. Locals in spiffy uniforms with epaulettes are poised nearby, eager to smooth your way. Private excursions in Mercedes buses with smoked glass glide away every few minutes. Dining room meals consist of "international cuisine," meaning you'll recognize everything. And don't forget to dress appropriately.

I say, avoid that cocoon. Select from among the zillion smaller, more personal, locally-owned lodging choices. The ten-room guesthouse in Ubud, Bali, looks like it was designed by the family-owners instead of from plans e-mailed in from London or Atlanta.

The people you meet are likely to be travelers keenly interested in local culture. Since there may be no dining room you'll be going out for meals with the potential for ethnic food and serendipitous conversations. On the way back, you may stop to hear some exotic music. You can stay for a month on what you'd spend in three days at the luxury palace. And what you spend will stay in the community rather than being shipped back to corporate headquarters.

Just because it's locally owned doesn't guarantee it's wonderful. Some are so awful they make great stories. But the good ones earn a warm place in your memory bank.

Rob Sangster is the author of the popular Traveler's Tool Kit: How to Travel Absolutely Anywhere. *It contains more than five hundred pages of Rob's road-tested information and advice on every aspect of independent world travel.*

GETTING OFF THE INDUSTRY PATH

As mentioned in Chapter 1, it's not easy to avoid the chain hotel cocoon. There are some big, powerful corporations constantly pushing you down that path. The big hotel chains are in bed with nearly everyone touching your trip, including the booking sites. They spend the equivalent of a small country's annual GDP in print advertising. It's just smart marketing—using their power and resources to gain a sustainable advantage. It's what the professors teach students to do in business school.

That doesn't mean you have to go along with it.

In all fairness, sometimes a chain hotel is truly the best choice in town, especially the exceptional chains where each and every property has its own personality (Oberoi, Orient-Express, and Amanresorts for example). Most of them are a different story. *The Wall Street Journal* noted in a late 2005 lodging story, "As hotel brands have proliferated and have been consolidated through mergers by big chains, it is increasingly difficult for consumers to tell them apart." So now the chains are battling to see who can add the most interesting amenities, such as satellite radio or quality stereo systems where you can plug in your own portable music player. Some of these corporate hotels do have enviable locations that can't be beat. Plus when you are able to cash in miles or points for a free room at a chain hotel, that's a deal in anyone's book.

In many cities, however, the name hotels cater to business travelers and are situated accordingly. They serve expense account road warriors and those taking a break from being expense account road warriors. (Lest you think I exaggerate, consider this fact: business travelers make up only 18% of total travel volume in the U.S., but generate one-third of travel industry revenue.) Many of the guests are in that hotel out of habit. They are paying for predictability. Nothing will surprise them and they won't mix with any strangers unless they want to.

I'm generalizing of course, but after reviewing hundreds of upscale hotels in a dozen countries for a travel trade publication, I can pretty accurately describe the typical guest. These are not the people you see wandering the back alleys, exploring the local market on their own, striking out on local transportation, or eating where the locals eat. While reviewing those fancy hotels, I have often simultaneously been staying at a local guesthouse or *pensione*. The contrast is striking. If you are staying at a Marriott or Hyatt, it's hard to leave home at home. The chain hotel guests I interview or overhear are talking about the stock market, their jobs, and how long they had to wait for their luggage to get to the room. The small hotel guests are talking about the funky restaurant they found for lunch, the people they met, and the amazing things they have seen and experienced in their travels.

Then there's the cost. As Rob Sangster noted in "Break Out of the Cocoon," you can routinely stay for a month in a city at a small independent hotel for the price of a few nights in the luxury palace. Worldwide, the average nightly room rate of a luxury hotel is over $250—not including taxes. If money is no object, negotiate a deal on the luxury palace and just follow the advice in the other chapters of this book to get more out of your trip. But if money does matter, look at it this way: two of you can stay at the business-like Park Tower in Buenos Aires for $300 a night, or you can bunk down at the Hostel-Inn Tango City for ten nights instead, with break- fast and free tango lessons thrown in the mix. You can stay at the penthouse suite for one night at the Fairmont in San Francisco—or use that money to hole up for *three months* at Hotel Diva. If you choose the latter option, nothing is stop- ping you from having a cocktail or two in the best hotel in town of course. That way you get to enjoy the ambiance guests are paying out the nose for, all for the cost of a few extra dollars on your bar tab.

When you commit to an independent hotel or even a villa, you're not taking the leap of faith you would have ten or twenty years ago. You still have to be wary of photographs: they can lie even better than they used to before the digital age. *SmartMoney* magazine once did a whole profile on hotel photographers and the tricks they use to make even the ugli- est property look fantastic. These deceptions included digital- ly enhanced grass, transplanted palm trees, and views from the best suite superimposed on the windows of a standard room. But now you can see what former guests have to say about hotels on sites such as TripAdvisor.com. If you use a travel agent, the good ones have a subscription to *Star Service*, which provides detailed and brutally honest reviews written by inspectors. Map programs can pinpoint your location, or even show you a satellite view of the hotel pool. Just doing a Google search will often turn up a variety of comments and reviews.

ECONOMICS ARE ON YOUR SIDE

Hotels like to give the illusion that they are worth a high price because of the experience they offer. After all, much of what you spend each night is going toward the fancy lobby, the gardens, the swimming pool, the renowned chef, and the spa—whether you take advantage of these amenities or not. In some cases, hotels have colluded to keep prices artificially high: six of the best hotels in Paris were fined close to a million dollars for agreeing to fix prices at a high level even when demand dropped. The hidden truth, however, is that we have a huge surplus of these hotels and more are coming online all the time. *Consumer Reports* estimates that in the U.S., 40% of the nation's supply of hotel rooms remains empty each night. Imagine what it's like in a country with fewer business travelers.

The Smiths would probably shrug at hearing all this and watch for a sale. The Johnsons will use this knowledge to get a better deal. They understand that an empty room is a room that makes no revenue. Only the most exclusive hotels are going to stay in a state of being half-empty just to keep their prices inflated. The others are going to quietly chop the rates to fill their rooms. They won't do this out in the open, however, unless it's through a special promotion: stay two nights, get one free for instance. Or a free suite upgrade and breakfast to fill a business hotel on a weekend.

They will usually sell these rooms through one of the following back channels:

- Priceline or Hotwire, where the hotel name is not revealed until the room is booked

- Site59 or LastMinuteTravel, where the room price is buried in a package deal

- A site such as SkyAuction.com, where excess inventory is auctioned off

- Standard air-and-hotel packages sold through travel agents, with lump-sum pricing

- Adventure tour packages sold through tour companies, with lump-sum pricing.

In nearly all these cases, the guest is paying half or less the standard rate.

I am a huge fan of Hotwire and Priceline. Combined I've probably used them fifty times. I don't use Priceline for flights: I don't like that much uncertainty in my schedule and the savings are seldom monumental. For hotels, however, I doubt I've ever paid more than 60% of the published rate by using this service or Hotwire. I've stayed in Courtyard Marriotts for under $40, in a nice downtown Sheraton for less than $60, and in a W Hotel in central Manhattan for $120, fees and taxes included. These were not isolated incidents—these kinds of deals are routine. You give up some things of course: you pick the area and hotel class, but not the actual property, so you don't know where you'll end up. You also won't get loyalty points. But the extra $50 or $100 per night you save is certainly worth it.

If you are on a fat company expense account and can build up loyalty points, book directly. If it's not your money, the premium you're paying will result in favorable treatment and points that are worth something. If you are on your own for expenses though, give yourself a huge discount and pocket the savings. To do it right, take advantage of two message boards devoted to bidding and buying on Priceline and Hotwire.

Some business owners I know will book through Hotwire or Priceline, then pay to upgrade to a suite upon arrival. If the hotel has an unfilled suite, management is happy to get the extra revenue. The guest is thrilled to get a premium room on the cheap. With a wink and a nod, everyone's pleased, yet the hotel still gets to keep posting its standard rates.

Outside the U.S., Priceline and Hotwire don't have much inventory yet and unfortunately there are no good international equivalents that I have found. Precision Reservations is the closest, selling off unbooked inventory mostly in Asia. Surf around, then use e-mail or the phone and contact the hotel directly. If the hotel is not near capacity, you can often work out a deal, especially if it's at the last minute. In the U.S., this doesn't work so well anymore with chain hotels—they're too locked into marketing agreements that keep them from doing direct discounts. The best you can usually hope for is an upgrade or a freebie to be thrown in.

One last piece of advice on hotel room purchases: beware of special package "deals" that are really no deal at all. SmarterTravel.com once did an investigative article on these special packages and found that in most cases, they're a marketing gimmick that's great for the hotel, but lousy for customers. A "Sports Fanatic" package at a Boston hotel, listed at $229, was $83 more than booking the room and buying the extras a la carte. Another hotel's "Stress-Free Shopping Package" in Chicago was even worse. The writer said, "Essentially, this package charges you an extra $90 to have a glass of wine and look at catalogs." Anything advertised as a "honeymoon deal" is almost sure to be more expensive than something you price out on your own.

LODGING ALTERNATIVES

Contrarian travelers know that hotels are often not the best choice for vacation lodging anyway. They look into villa or condo rentals, home exchanges, and park cabins. This is especially important for a family. A standard hotel room is a terrible place for a family to spend a vacation. There's never enough room for all the baggage a family carries and the close quarters start amplifying tensions in no time. If it is necessary to stay in a hotel room, perhaps to take advantage of a huge resort complex, then find a way to upgrade to a suite or get adjoining rooms. Otherwise you'll need a vacation from your vacation when you return.

A better bet is to find a way to get a whole apartment or house. Smart travelers know that this can be cheaper than a hotel when stretched out over a week or two and there will be ten times the space. You'll have real closets, a full kitchen, a living room, and more. In nearly any vacation area, there are plenty of these places to rent, often by vacation homeowners who are just looking for a little extra income. Even in Manhattan or Paris you can find an apartment to rent, for less than a hotel if you'll be there for a week. In state and national parks, families or groups can rent a whole cabin for less than the price of two budget motel rooms.

If you have a house or apartment of your own, why not leverage that and bring your lodging costs down to nothing?

If you live in a popular tourist area yourself, you can join a home exchange program and stay in places near and far by doing a swap. You stay in someone else's house for a week or a month, they stay in yours, and both parties save hundreds or thousands of dollars.

Home Exchanges: The Best Way to Go
by Larry Habegger

I did my first home exchange last summer and it was the best travel arrangement I ever made. I wanted to take my family of four (two daughters, ages seven and four) to Paris for a month, but the prospect of finding a hotel that could accommodate us for a price that wouldn't wipe out my life savings gave me a headache. But if I could find a Parisian family that wanted to spend a month in San Francisco at the same time I wanted to be in Paris, I could have an apartment in Paris at no cost, plus have someone to watch over my place and take care of my two cats.

I signed up with an agency six months before departure but decided to cover all bases and put a listing on Craigslist.com as well. As the weeks rolled on I saw lots of nice places in Paris and elsewhere on the agency site (one in Rome was so tempting we almost changed our plans), but none quite matched our needs, or ours theirs. I was just beginning to worry that I wouldn't find a match and my long-planned trip to Paris would become camping in California when I got an e-mail from a man named Jacques in Paris. He'd seen our listing on Craig's List and liked what he saw. The dates were about right. He had an apartment in the 20th arrondisement, near Père Lachaise cemetery, a block from a

Metro stop. The apartment was modern, full of light, with an inner courtyard and friendly neighbors.

My place is on Telegraph Hill, a short walk from many of San Francisco's main attractions, with a view of the bay. Their place was a little larger than ours, but they had only one child (a daughter, age nine), and they loved cats.

Over the next few weeks we had a flurry of e-mails, exchanging photos, recommendations, ideas for the visit, suggestions for how to make the most of our respective neighborhoods. We had so much e-mail that we never actually spoke to each other by phone until after we'd agreed to the exchange and were in each other's apartments!

When we arrived we found the place to be everything Jacques had promised: secure, clean, airy, in a lively Paris neighborhood. Jacques and his family, too, were delighted with our hillside aerie, and it's safe to say we all had a fabulous experience. It was so good that we became friends and plan to swap homes again sometime.

What did we get for it? A free place to live, with all the comforts of home, including space to spread out. Toys for my girls to play with, and for Jacques's daughter in our house. Familiarity with a Paris neighborhood that began to feel like home because we had great recommendations from a local family. A carefree base for my family in a foreign city. And, someone to mind our home, take care of our cats, and make sure all was well when we returned.

Some people worry about valuables, invasion of their space, and other unnamed concerns. For me, swapping a home is the best way to travel if you intend to explore one city. You have a base of operations at no more than the cost of your housing at home and instant familiarity with a new neighborhood. And, for those worried about strangers in their home, remember that you are in their home, too, and you both have a vested interest in taking care of the place. And when it's all said and done, you can spend a month in Paris and hang onto your life savings.

Is an agency better than Craig's List? Hard to say. The agency gives you someone to fall back on if you have a bad experience, but Craig's List is built on trust. An agency has a nominal membership fee and Craig's List is free. I've found subletters and rented apartments many times through Craig's List and I've never had a bad experience. It all depends on your comfort level. The main thing is, don't be afraid to exchange your home: you won't regret it.

Larry Habegger is executive editor of Travelers' Tales. He teaches travel writing and leads writers workshops at home and abroad, and swaps his San Francisco apartment with families from other lands whenever possible.

There are plenty of other unconventional options. If you are a couple exploring Europe, think about traveling on one of the river cruise boats. Unlike a conventional cruise, they are small and don't float on an endless sea. They dock at towns in the French wine country or at castles in Hungary, providing both transportation and lodging in one.

If you want to see the great outdoors, skip the roadside motels and look into park lodges and cabins. Besides being a great value, they put you right in the middle of things, rather than driving distance away. In mountain areas of Switzerland, Italy, and Nepal, you can hike from lodge to lodge (or hut to hut), waking up with a view that will glow in your mind forever.

If you have a long stretch to travel overland, consider an overnight train journey. You've covered lodging and transportation with one expense.

HOW TO FIND ALTERNATIVE LODGING

"How do I find a place to stay if it's not on Expedia or Orbitz?" In all seriousness, someone I met in a hotel bar once asked me this question. This was no travel novice either; it was someone who traveled a good twenty nights a year on business and took one or two family vacations each year. But on every one of those trips, he traveled like a sheep.

Here are a few ways to get beyond the obvious. Consider these strategies as places to start and then branch out from there.

ALTERNATIVE HOTELS

Many backpackers travel around the world for a year or two without ever making a hotel reservation. They show up, take a look around, and get a room that meets their needs. More on that subject in Chapter 9.

Guidebooks are a good source for finding small, independent hotels. Buy one or more, or check several out from your local library to get a broader view. Each has its own target audience and point of view. For specific types of places, such as bed-and-breakfast inns in North America or Europe, you can find several good directories in book form and on the internet. Several hostel sites feature details, customer reviews, rates, and availability.

Locally run web sites in your destination are a great source as well. I've used region-specific sites to find some great hotel gems: AndeanTravelWeb.com for Peru, for example, or YucatanToday.com for the area around Mérida, Mexico. The key is that both of these offer unbiased listings—they are not a booking service trying to steer you to specific properties. TripAdvisor.com is a great source of customer reviews for larger hotels; VirtualTourist.com has reviews on many smaller hotels, hostels, and guesthouses.

If you prefer to use a travel agent, try to find one who knows a lot about where you are going, ideally a specialist in the region. He or she will often know about the off-the-radar places that don't show up in every Sunday newspaper story and airline magazine.

Another great method to find wonderful hotels is to just ask. People who have already been to a place will have some knowledge. People who live there will usually know even more. If you are going diving somewhere, call or e-mail a dive shop and ask where you should stay. If a friend of a friend has moved there, get in touch with him or her. If you read a good article that listed a variety of reasonable lodging choices (and didn't just rave about one fancy resort), stick it in a file and then check the hotels' web sites when you are getting ready to book the trip.

HALF-PRICE HOTELS

As mentioned earlier, use Priceline and Hotwire, but in conjunction with Better Bidding and BiddingForTravel so you won't put more money on the table than is needed. Also watch for deals on sale announcement sites such as TravelZoo. You'll often see bargain basement sales on hotel rooms in popular areas. If it's the last minute, go to a site that specializes in clearing out last-minute inventory. In notoriously overbuilt areas—such as Las Vegas and Bangkok—there's no reason to ever pay anything close to full price unless there is a specific hotel you absolutely love.

Apartment and Villa Rentals

There are dozens of web sites that list houses, condos, and apartments for rent. Put "Tuscany villas" in a search engine and you'll see what I mean. The largest international property listing sites are in the resources section on my web site (www.ContrarianTraveler.com), but many areas have locally run sites with even more choices. Spend some time searching to get a good feel for prices and what will work best.

Home Exchanges

Home exchanges are a great way to leverage your empty apartment or house at a time when it's going to be empty anyway. If you're especially frugal and you want to connect with other like minds, use Craigslist.com. It's free and you can target specific cities where you want to exchange. For more peace of mind and far better luck, join a formal home exchange program. These have a formal framework and more serious exchangers. There are a half-dozen large memberships and a few devoted to specific niches, such as singles. Nose around their sites and browse the listings to decide which one is a good match.

You pay an annual fee and you post details about your home, where you would like to go, and usually a few photos. You can actively request exchanges with other members or just wait for offers to roll in. If you live in Amsterdam or Miami Beach, you'll get more offers than you can possibly entertain. If you live on a farm in Iowa, you'll have to work much harder before finding a match.

Free Lodging

Yes, with a little legwork you can actually pay nothing for a place to rest your head. It may sound crazy, but there are plenty of hospitable souls around the world who will be glad to let you come spend a few nights in their home. Several organizations revolve around the theory that travelers will stay with hosts when they travel, then be a host themselves when they are back home.

The original hospitality exchange program was Servas, which is still very active, promoting cultural exchange and understanding. It is obvious from the names of the others that they have less lofty goals: GlobalFreeloaders, Hospitality Exchange, and CouchSurfers. In my backpacker days my wife and I stayed with several hosts. Now that we are more grounded, we have hosted newfound friends from Australia, Canada, Scotland, and Brazil. As a traveler, if it's your first time in a city, this can be a terrific way to get on the insider track and to meet people who aren't connected with tourism.

Lodging Questions for the Contrarian Traveler

1. Is a standard hotel the best bet for this trip? Is there another option that will provide more space or more comfort?

2. If a hotel makes the most sense, are you getting the best value for what you are spending?

3. Do you like to have a room that looks just like the one in your hometown, or would you rather stay in a place with more character?

4. Can you leverage your house or apartment and exchange it for lodging in another location?

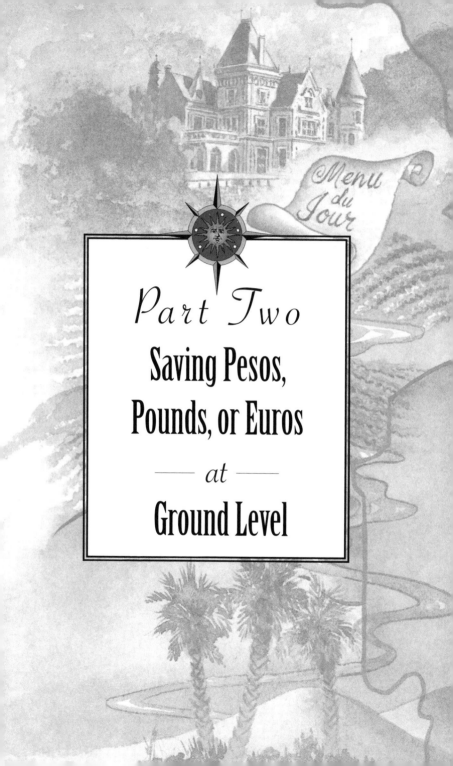

Part Two

Saving Pesos, Pounds, or Euros

— *at* —

Ground Level

6

CONTRARIAN DINING

See Where the Tourists Are Eating, Then Go Elsewhere

"If you reject the food, ignore the customs, fear the religion, and avoid the people, you might better stay home. You are like a pebble thrown into water; you become wet on the surface but you are never a part of the water."

—James A. Michener

When the Smiths sit down for a meal in a strange land, they are driven by unease and fear. They have heard tales of sheep's brains, dog steaks, and grilled guinea pig in adventure travel stories and want no chance of encountering any of that. They are scared that the waiter won't understand what they are ordering in English, but don't want to be bothered carrying around a phrase book or dictionary in the local language. Even though they can't see the kitchen in international chain restaurants and hotel dining rooms, they eat there because they think it won't make them sick. (Somehow, one or the other usually gets diarrhea anyway.) They seldom stray from areas where most tourists are gathered and confine most of their dining choices to what they have seen in their guidebook or in magazine articles. If they become friendly with a local person who then invites them to have lunch at his or her house, the Smiths politely decline.

No matter where they go in their own country or around the world, they seldom get beyond slight variations on the familiar. When a neighbor asks, "How was the food?" upon their return, the reply is predictable: "Not too bad."

When the Johnsons sit down for a meal in a strange place, it's another part of their adventure. They read up on local specialties before arriving and find out what dishes are seasonal treats. They savor the fresh ingredients that go into food at market stall restaurants and watch as their meal is being prepared. They always carry a phrase book or dictionary so they can decipher the local restaurant menus. When deciding where to dine, they frequently ask local residents for recommendations. They stroll neighborhoods well away from the tourist district and often pop into small local restaurants on a whim. If they become friendly with a local resident who invites them to his or her home, the Johnsons find a way to fit it into their schedule, knowing it will probably be one of the most memorable meals of their trip.

Because of their willingness to experiment and ask around, the Johnsons retain vivid memories of the meals they have had in this foreign place—whether it's Budapest, Bombay, or Boston. When a neighbor asks, "How was the food?" upon their return, the Johnsons hardly know where to start.

According to a study by the U.S. Department of Labor, food and drinks comprise a larger part of the travel budget, on average, than any other category. According to their figures, 25% to 28% of a vacation's cost goes to dining and drinking, a bigger portion than airfare, lodging, entertainment, or local transportation. So why settle for humdrum meals you could be eating in your hometown?

INSTITUTIONS ARE INSTITUTIONAL

Most of the year I live in Nashville, Tennessee, a city of about a million people that is the frequent subject of magazine travel articles and TV travel shows. Most of the writers and TV hosts who breeze through follow a well-worn path that doesn't require much digging. One particular restaurant in my city has been featured on two cooking shows, in three major magazines, and in two of the country's largest newspapers. It's not the best restaurant in town, but it certainly has the best publicist. After all this press and attention, everyone assumes it must be the place to go, so it is constantly packed, especially with out-of-town visitors. Service is indifferent and the waits are long, but it doesn't matter. The place has become an institution.

Throughout the world, this bandwagon tendency is repeated, causing popular "must-visit" restaurants to become expensive and mobbed, while other excellent establishments remain local secrets. You probably know of an institution like this in your own hometown if you get many tourists, or you have probably eaten at a place like this and felt disappointed afterwards. Despite its reputation as "the place to go," it didn't live up to your expectations. One *Condé Nast Traveler* food writer could have been writing about many of these places when he said of a Bejing institution, "The prices are high, the food simplistic, and the service non-existent..." He summed it up saying the well-known restaurant "has been open to the public since 1925. Its time is up."

The Wall Street Journal published a rundown of America's ten most overrated restaurants. On the list were a few storied institutions that are coasting on their laurels. For Peter Luger's Steak House in New York, the review mentioned the charmless waiters, predatory neighborhood youths, and the fact you can't use a credit card. "Why do reasonable people go through this exercise in masochism?" they asked. For Joe's Stone Crab in Miami, they noted that the crabs arrive at the restaurant precooked. On Restaurant 66 in New York, they said "it churns out pallid versions of classics that you can find for a lot less in Chinatown." The last one is the most common problem with these places: better food is often just a short cab ride or walk away.

To Market, To Market!
by Richard Sterling

As usual, the first thing I did upon landing in Hong Kong was to check the local entertainment rag for any news of my favorite restaurants. I anxiously flipped through the pages, hoping for the best possible news. But damn! There it was in black and white and a four color, half page photo. Not only was the Pigeon Shack being written of, it was being written of by that fancy boy that people simply must slavishly follow. The Pigeon Shack was doomed. The food would still be good for a while, but already the service was suffering. They weren't used to handling such crowds. They were giddy with the big tips and already getting uppity about it. The cute waitress was flirting with businessmen and the waiter was getting surly because he couldn't do likewise. The only thing that could have hastened the joint's demise would be if it were suddenly bestowed with a sweeping view of the harbor.

As a general rule, popular restaurants are not popular because they have great food at great prices. They are popular because they are popular. People go to them because people go to them. Or because they have a great sweeping view of the harbor. Fie on popular places! Down, down to hell with 'em! They cost too much anyway. And on the travel circuit, those joints have a tendency to "internationalize" themselves, or start serving some horrible thing called "fusion." Fusion is something nuclear, and to be avoided. Such places lose touch with their roots. They no longer taste of where they are.

For true local flavor and the best price, get your hungry self to the market. Caveat emptor: I am not suggesting that travelers to the USA visit the snack bar at Wal-Mart, or dine at the mini-market of the local gas station. You'll get a true local taste, all right, but you'll regret it. But throughout most of the world, especially in areas like East Asia, the Mediterranean, Latin America, go to the market. The noodle stalls and the barbeque shacks and the soup sellers and even that guy offering fried snake, these are the people who know best about what's good. They see it first, as it arrives at the *souk* or the *mercado* or the *cho*. They have first pick. And they know their onions! And they are cooking for people they see every day, people who will complain and take their business to the next stall if it don't satisfy. The price is always the best for you because they get the best price for the goods, as they bypass the middleman. And they don't pay outrageous rent for a sweeping view of the harbor. But they have a better view: the market itself.

In traditional societies everybody goes to the market. In some countries they go two, even three, times per day. This is a place where life unfolds before your eyes. All classes of people come here and interact, barter, visit, argue, cuss, and discuss. All forms of human intercourse but the sexual (invitations thereto notwithstanding) can be observed. Who needs the harbor, or the high prices? To market, to market!

Richard Sterling is the principal author of Lonely Planet's World Food series. Known as the "Indiana Jones of Gastronomy," his most recent book is How to Eat Around the World.

Your taste buds are going on vacation, too. Let them live a little! The Smiths go away year after year, but eat only at tourist restaurants and hotel buffets. You can often find them dining in a chain restaurant that is a familiar name from home. They have no idea what kinds of culinary delights lie two or three streets over. Wherever they go, they end up with a mix of familiar fare they're used to and watered-down imitations of local cuisine. From trip to trip, the buffet table in one country looks very similar to one in another.

Whenever you see interviews or magazine stories that ask chefs and food writers about their most memorable meals, tourist restaurants and these dining institutions are never on the list. Instead, the chef or food writer will invariably gush on about some little French bistro on a back street of Paris, a Chiang Mai street stall cooking up Thai food at midnight, or some rickety beach hut in the tropics serving up fresh fish on banana leaves. This is not because these chefs and food writers are all cheapskate bohemians at heart. They are well-paid professionals and often they are traveling on a fat expense account on top of it. They seek out these lesser-known places because the food is fresher and more authentic. The people preparing the meals really care whether you like their cooking or not. The menu prices reflect the ingredients and the effort, not the marketing skill or the marble floor.

Granted, if you are a gourmet foodie who enjoys fine dining at every meal, with raspberry drizzles and flower petals on your plate, back alley eateries and market stalls are probably not going to be your thing. (A recent article in a luxury travel magazine gallingly said the second-largest city in Slovakia had "no hotels or restaurants worth mentioning.")

Still, even if money is no object, the concept of getting beyond the obvious is still very important. High-end restaurants come and go with alarming frequency and what's in your guidebook or that *Times* article you cut out last year is probably out of date. Often the hot place to go last year is now without that chef that made it so hot. Ask locals with good taste which places are the best right now. Ask a concierge and tell him not to just send you to what's popular. Ask the chef at a restaurant you enjoyed.

BECOME A REGULAR FOR A WEEK

Actually, if you had a meal you really enjoyed, near where you are staying, then go back. Most of us feel this need when traveling to try as many different places as possible, with the lure of a new atmosphere and menu always tugging at our sleeve. This despite the fact we have only sampled a small fraction of what the restaurant we just went to has on its menu.

We don't go out to a different restaurant every single time we eat at home and it doesn't make much sense to do that elsewhere either. If a meal was really good and you liked the atmosphere, go back again—and take a few friends. After the second or third time, an interesting thing will probably happen: you'll get better treatment. Appetizers or after-dinner drinks may show up gratis. You may get shown to the best table. The owners themselves may come over to ask how your meal went. Business owners value loyalty and reward it accordingly. After a couple of meals, you'll also know what's best to order.

WET YOUR WHISTLE WITH SOMETHING DIFFERENT

Almost anywhere in the world you can buy a Pepsi or Coke. At almost any decently-stocked bar in the world, you can get a Jack Daniels, a Johnny Walker, or a Heineken beer. But why would you?

After sight, taste is the sense that is most tantalized when we travel. It's a globalized world we're in, with more Starbucks outlets in London than in New York or Seattle. But just because you can eat and drink the same things while traveling that you would at home doesn't mean you should. Even disregarding the unimaginative nature of keeping your food and drink routine intact, drinking something shipped across an ocean or land mass costs you more money. In Argentina, you could buy for the same price a glass of French wine, a glass of imported beer, or a whole *bottle* of great local Malbec wine. A Pisco Sour in Peru will cost half what an import cocktail does. The same with rum in any country that grows sugar cane—it's $2 a pint for the cheap stuff and $4 for the good stuff in the Philippines. Vodka is cheaper than bottled water almost anywhere between Moscow and Warsaw. Some of the best beer in the world is two pints for a dollar in Eastern Europe. Local soda and juice brands are usually far cheaper than a Coke, even when the latter is bottled locally.

Wherever you are traveling, the next state over or the other side of the world, find out what the local specialties are and make them part of your adventure. Have some ice wine in Ontario, some Riesling wine in upstate New York, a Lone Star beer in Texas, or a Yazoo beer in Nashville. Grab an Inca Kola in Cusco, a Mekong Whiskey cocktail in Bangkok, a fresh coconut milk in the tropics, or a sweet *lassi* in Jaipur. With wineries popping up all over the world, you can find something locally produced almost anywhere. They won't all be great, but some will be a pleasant surprise.

Charles Leocha, author of *Ski Europe*, noted in one of his

articles that a central facet of the European ski experience is sampling the particular warm-up drink of choice served from slopeside huts. In Austria you will find Jägertee, "a warm and delicious concoction of tea, spices, and a high-powered Austrian rum called Strohs." In Germany it's Glühwein, hot red wine with cloves and other spices, spiked with a local schnapps. Grappa in Italy, the kirsch-spiked Café Fertig in Switzerland, or throughout the Alps, Obstler—a schnapps made from fall fruits. Drinking a boring plain coffee or a cold soda seems almost an affront to the mountains.

GET OUT OF THE BOXES

Don't forget that there are plenty of places to grab food or a snack apart from a restaurant. Reasonable hygiene rules apply, but it can be a lot of fun to sample what's on offer elsewhere. If you are fortunate enough to be invited to someone's home, take advantage of it. You will likely taste things that aren't on any restaurant menu and can learn something about local customs in the process.

If you have access to a kitchen, spend some leisurely time in a local grocery store and buy some things you wouldn't get at home—especially local fruit and vegetables in season. A grocery store is often where you find a foreign country's most dramatic bargains (except in Japan, where even an apple seems shockingly expensive).

In a city, wander around and see where most people are eating. Get away from the obvious tourist zone; even in the U.S. these are the priciest areas. The Times Square area of New York City is brutal for your wallet. Locals mostly avoid the Fisherman's Wharf area of San Francisco. In resort areas, however, there's even more of a disparity. You can easily spend $50 each on a so-so meal for two on Paradise Island in the Bahamas, or walk across the bridge to New Providence Island and get a fresh conch fritter meal with a beer for less than $10. Hardly any Cancun tourist leaves the beach area to hop a local bus to where all the Mexicans are, but the ones that do find tastier food at family restaurants spilling out onto the sidewalks.

In transit, you see another side of a country's cuisine. "This is Turkish fast food," my seatmate said as he shared his fried dough balls on a bus from Bursa to Istanbul. This led to a conversation about eating habits and holidays that went on for an hour.

"These are the best samosas in town," an Indian college professor said to me as we ate food from a little train station stall in Madras. We went on to talk about vegetarian customs and why people of European ancestry are more likely to go bald.

These encounters, and many others like them, were a different take on breaking bread together, ones that opened up to long conversations as we left the respective stations and moved along to our destination. Time in transit can be an interesting study in eating habits. You may not want to eat some of the things on offer—I never got used to the smells of dried squid and steamed silkworm larvae at bus stops in Korea when I lived there—but it is a nice contrast to the chain food culture we see at home.

WHAT IF I CAN'T EAT THIS STUFF?

Up to now, I haven't said a word about dietary restrictions. It's not because I'm not sensitive to it: my father is diabetic and my wife doesn't eat meat. The problem is, there are so many kinds of restrictions to discuss. Plus there is such a different climate in different regions. Being a vegetarian is perfectly normal in southern India, but unheard of in many other places, for example. You will have to do some homework on your own situation. The common thread is that you will need to do a little more advance planning and you will need to carry a dictionary or phrase book when in a country where English is not the first language. If in a foreign culture (which for vegetarians could mean Texas), understand that your requirements might be met with puzzlement. Be insistent when necessary. Be doubly insistent when there's an allergy involved.

In some places, "I don't eat meat," means you still eat chicken. People on an island will think you're from outer space when you say you don't eat seafood. Asking if something is spicy might not get you very far in a place where nothing is considered spicy unless it is loaded with habañeros. Something like lactose or gluten intolerance will be met with a blank stare in much of the world. Carry some extra snacks for when you run into trouble spots and see if you can get accommodations with a kitchen.

Restrictions don't automatically mean you have to eat boring hotel food. I have included some helpful dining resources at ContrarianTraveler.com.

Dining Questions for the Contrarian Traveler

1. Is your fear of the unknown driving you to eat boring, predictable meals while on vacation?

2. Do you gravitate to tourist and hotel restaurants out of habit, rather than exploring beyond the few blocks near your hotel?

3. Do you ask locals and other travelers for dining advice—or do you just go by what's in magazines or your guidebook?

4. Have you been to the local market?

5. Think of the most memorable meal from your travels. Where was it? How could you duplicate that experience in other places?

7

CONTRARIAN GROUND TRANSPORTATION

Suckers for Wheels and Wheels for Suckers

"The interstate highway system is a wonderful thing. It makes it possible to go from coast to coast without seeing anything or meeting anybody."

—Charles Kuralt, *A Life on the Road*

When the Smiths go on vacation and venture beyond where they are staying, they travel in one of three ways: a rental car, a taxi from the hotel, or on a guided tour bus. On their trips to London and New York, they spent hundreds of dollars on taxis. They thought Mexico would be cheaper, but the taxi rides and escorted bus tours to the ruins caused them to go way over budget. When they rented a car in Europe, they got charged a fortune for scratches—even though they bought the insurance—and found additional supplemental charges on their credit card when they got home. When they last took a cruise, the organized shore excursions ended up costing them almost as much as the cruise itself.

When the Johnsons go on vacation, they travel by a dozen

or more methods, depending on what is appropriate for the situation. When they go somewhere like London, New York, or Seoul, nearly all of their trips are on the subway. When they went down to Mexico, they spent one-third of what the Smiths did by taking advantage of the excellent local bus system. They toured Hanoi all day by bicycle rickshaw. The Johnsons have traveled through Thailand, Turkey, and Egypt without ever renting a car. They have biked through national parks and hiked through the Alps. The one time the Johnsons took a cruise, they arranged shore excursions locally and chopped two-thirds off the cruise line prices.

There are a lot of ways to get around out there. Most of them are a better value than what the tourist herds are using. Look for alternate ways to get from Point A to Point B and you will save a small fortune, with a more interesting experience as a bonus.

Renting a Car Is a Last Resort

Americans have a deep love of automobiles that goes back generations. Most of us see a car as something akin to a wallet or purse: life without one for even a day is cause for panic. The way our country has been developed, with nearly every town a collection of strip malls and parking lots, it's hard to function without your own wheels. So when we go somewhere that is going to require any moving around, we automatically assume we need a rental car. Airports near ski resorts thrive on this attitude, renting out lots full of cars that are mostly going to sit idle at a resort (and renting SUVs to gullible vacationers who think they'll need four-wheel drive to get around). Having grown up in a country where "urban planning" and "density development" are seen as something propagated by communists, we figure any place we go is going to require our own car. Before you assume that a rental car will be necessary, however, do a little digging and make sure.

Renting a car can make a lot of sense sometimes. If you have rented a villa in a remote area and are carrying kids and groceries, there may not be another viable option. If you are traveling from country inn to country inn around Ireland, a car is going to make it a whole lot easier. If you want to really see the Grand Canyon instead of just making a quick stop or two, driving along the rim is going to be much more satisfying than other methods. American and Canadian vacations in general are hard to pull off without a vehicle.

In much of the world, however, especially outside the sprawl-happy U.S., you can do most of what there is to do and see most of what there is to see without ever getting behind your own steering wheel. As a result, you will spend far less money.

Besides the cost of the vehicle, there are plenty of charges on top to consider when you rent a car. In many cases you don't need to purchase additional insurance, but rental car companies push it hard—they make 15% to 20% of their revenue from these charges. In many foreign countries, however, your normal insurance policy and credit card backup don't apply, so you're taking a risk if you don't spend the extra $20 to $40 per day. Then there are tolls. A trip from Paris to Marseille will cost a whopping $115 in tolls. The toll road from Cancun to Mérida in Mexico is $25. A trip down the turnpike from New York City to Washington, D.C will have you reaching for your wallet regularly. These all pale in comparison to Japan, where a two-hour trip can result in toll charges of $40 or more and driving from one end of the country to the other costs $330.

Don't forget parking charges: nonexistent in rural and suburban areas, but a hefty extra in cities. Then there is the cost of gasoline, which is historically high in most of the world, downright outrageous in Europe. (You can mitigate this somewhat by renting a fun little two-seater Smart Car in Europe.) In plenty of routes around the world, you can now fly somewhere for less than it would cost to rent a car and drive yourself.

On top of all that, tourists in Europe seem to have more problems with rental car companies than anything else. If you read many travel magazines where people write in with problems, after a while you get the impression that extra charges that show up on your credit card once home are an integral part of the car companies' revenue streams.

DRIVING IS DANGEROUS

Yes, we've all heard horror stories about a bus going over the side of a mountain or a train derailment killing hundreds. These fatalities are a small drop in the bucket, however, compared to the number of people killed each day behind the wheel of a car. Nearly 43,000 people die on U.S. roads each year and most of those people are close to home, meaning they know the route, the vehicle, and the road conditions. Imagine the amplified risk if none of these factors are in place, if you are driving on an unfamiliar route, in a rented vehicle, with road conditions and signs that are a mystery. Now imagine that you are driving on the other side of the road on top of it. Sound risky? Probably so, but thousands of people do just that each year in just the U.K. alone. Some of them end up in the hospital. Many more end up with costs and insurance hassles resulting from fender benders.

THE PROBLEM WITH TOUR BUSES

Tour buses serve a purpose. They're reliable. They're air-conditioned. They have a bathroom. They have a public address system that allows a tour guide to drone on about what you are seeing outside the windows. Their main benefit, however, is that they allow the tour operator to corral everyone together and get the economies of scale necessary for a sustainable tour business. They can get group rates on admissions, negotiate deals with large tourist restaurants, and get a commission from those shopping plazas you will inevitably stop at over and over. They can use the same driver and guide every time, so it's all predictable and free of surprises.

Unfortunately, this means your experience will also be fully predictable and free of surprises. If you want to just hit the main sights, click your photo, and be on to the next sight, tour buses work well. If you are looking for anything more, or would like some choice in where you eat lunch or buy souvenirs, you are out of luck. The hard pill to swallow, either way, is that you are paying a large premium for becoming one of the sheep. In nearly every case, you could do far better arranging the trip on your own, ending up with much more control over what you see and do as well. If you're willing to go down a few notches on the comfort scale, you can do it all for a tenth of the price and come back with stories that can be told for a lifetime.

Seeing a Culture Through Its Transportation
by Marie Javins

If you travel to meet people and experience local culture, get off the tour bus and onto the public one.

Locals don't take overland trucks or luxury coach tours. They don't shield themselves from the world in private taxis. They take whatever transport is available in their home country. The poorer the region—and the fewer private cars—the more likely there is to be accessible, cheap public transportation.

It won't be comfortable in most cases, and you may find yourself wishing for a flat tire just so you have time to pee. At some point you will surely crave the "tourist bubble" and organized timetable that comes from floating along in private transport, but when you look back at you time with the masses, you will embrace the chaos and color of your once-in-a-lifetime experience.

I have ridden in Peugeots with comedic Masai warriors—they bantered throughout the two-hour journey. Unfortunately, it was all in Swahili and all I could understand was the laughter of the Kenya-bound audience. I have seen Jackie Chan movies on buses all over the world—physical comedy is universal—but my favorite viewing was in Botswana, where young Botswanan men chanted "Jackie, Jackie" at the climax.

On a sleeper train in China, a marathon mahjong game went on at my feet from sunup to sundown. On a local train in Kazakhstan, a grandma listened intently to a translation of what I was doing there, then gave me the thumbs-up along with a huge smile. A swarthy Uzbek popped an Abba tape into the bus cassette deck somewhere near Bukhara, and nearly the whole bus sang along.

In Uganda, I inadvertently boarded the school bus one morning after flagging down the public minibus. It stopped next in front of a small school, where a teacher gave some coins to the conductor before ushering six uniformed children to the bus. The conductor got off and lifted the smallest children onto the first seat. As we approached each child's home, the child would squeak for the driver to stop. The conductor would then help the child off of the bus. In one case, he ushered the kids across the busy street while the other passengers waited patiently.

Going by local transport is not without risk. Your luggage will get dusty. You may inhale diesel fumes and secondhand smoke. Your knees may hurt for weeks afterwards, and it is entirely possible that you might end up in a vehicle accident. You will encounter toilets of nightmares. But you will also inter-act with the local culture that you left home to experience. You'll be on the same level as the people you came to see, instead of staring at them through a camera lens. You might even find yourself asked to explain Tupac Shakur to a Siberian waiter, or in Sumbawa learning the finer points of the Koran from a Javanese bartender from Guam. And best of all? You'll get all this for the price of a National Geographic DVD rental back home.

Marie Javins is a writer and comic book colorist who took local trans-portation around the world for an entire year in 2001. Her recent book, Stalking the Wild Dik-dik, *is about the Cape Town to Cairo leg of that trip. She is also the author of* Best in Tent Camping: New Jersey, *and is transportation contributing editor at GoNOMAD.com.*

RIDING WITH THE LOCALS

I traveled and lived in Turkey for nearly six months and never got behind the wheel of a car. I lived in South Korea for over a year and never once used my international driver's license. In my three yearlong trips backpacking around the world, I rented a car three times: in Jordan, Guam, and

Saipan. In every case it was because I had an assignment that required covering a lot of ground in a hurry. No, I didn't hitchhike and no, I didn't skip places because I couldn't get to them. I just traveled the way people who live there travel instead of how foreign tourists travel. It doesn't take long to realize this is not only cheap and easy, it can also be a much more enriching way to experience a foreign culture.

Local transportation is a great window into a culture. By sitting side-by-side with people who live there, you are on their level. You see what they see. When I rode the local bus system from one end of Israel to the other, I saw the country's people in an unvarnished way: brusque to the point of comedy, and carrying automatic weapons as casually as they carried their cell phones (the army kids, of course). You can't come close to understanding India until you ride their train system: millions of people on the move with the largest employer in the world. If you manage to go by all three classes, you can see the caste system and levels of education on display in ways that can't be conveyed in a book. A ride on the Shinkansen bullet train in Japan is a fascinating study in Japanese cultural habits, with a ride on the subway at rush hour providing an amazing contrast.

Taking alternative transportation can be uncomfortable at times, but comfort and value are not mutually exclusive. Alternatives to taxis and tour buses are not limited to chicken buses in third-world countries. You can get a double-decker bus from London to Glasgow for as little as $3 if booked well in advance, less than $20 the day of departure. A nice bus from one end of South Korea to the other is under $30. A top-of-the-line bus in Mexico, with three seats across and loads of legroom, is only about $6 to $8 per hour of travel.

You can get a first class sleeper train from Bangkok to Chiang Mai, Thailand for about $35.

SKIPPING THE CAB LINE

Much of the time, taxis can be a wonderful thing. They can get you from your hotel to a restaurant for a few bucks, or can take you all around for a day for less than what it would cost to drive yourself. At airports, however, they can be a budget killer. In some cities, such as New York, local governments have realized that gouging tourists is bad for business and they have instituted flat-rate pricing. Others haven't gotten that message though and the taxi prices are downright predatory, either officially or in practice. In some cities, the price of going to the airport is one-third of what it costs to go *from* the airport. In some cities in Europe, it's going to cost you $100 no matter which way you're going.

Finding an alternative to taxis can save both money and time. Trains serving Newark and Philadelphia airports, for example, are far faster and cheaper than taking a cab. The Heathrow Express trains in London cost one-third the price of a taxi and get there in fifteen minutes from Paddington Station. Singapore's metro system goes right to the airport for only $2. The train from Narita Airport to downtown Tokyo is $25 to $50 depending on class, but that's a pretty good deal compared to $180 and up for a taxi! In many cities, shuttle buses run from the airport to hotel districts for a fraction of the cost of a taxi and some hotels will provide a complimentary ride: check when booking. If you stay at a Disney-owned hotel in Orlando, they'll even give you special tags to put on your luggage so you can go right past baggage claim, hop on the shuttle, and have your bags delivered to your hotel.

PASSING UP THE SHORE EXCURSION

There is not a lot about cruises in this book, mostly because there are few variables there that can save you money and enrich your experience. You are all in it together—the hundreds of you—with few opportunities to avoid the herd mentality. Here is one tip that will save you a fortune, however: Don't sign up for any shore excursions. Whatever it is they are offering, you can do it yourself for far less. According to a study done by *The Wall Street Journal*, cruise line markups on shore excursions range from a low of 20% up to well over 100%. Like rental car companies profiting from unnecessary insurance charges and hotels profiting from overpriced phone calls and internet access charges, these markups represent a significant ongoing revenue source.

When booking the cruise, look at these organized shore excursions as a last resort. Plunk down the cost of a good guidebook for where you are going instead or borrow one from a library. Between this and a little web research at sites such as CruiseCritic.com, you'll likely find plenty of local operators at port who can offer the same excursion. Hiring a car and driver for the day will be cheaper than an organized bus trip, but with a better lunch stop and fewer obligatory shopping stops. One expert noted in a *SmartMoney* magazine article that bus excursions in many Caribbean ports are four or five times the cost of just taking a local taxi for the same trip.

THE JOURNEY IS THE POINT

The transportation from one spot to the next can actually be the main draw of the trip. Adventure tour catalogs are full of options: week-long river-rafting trips, cross-country skiing from inn to inn, biking in a loop around a scenic area, or long-term hiking through mountains.

You don't necessarily have to spend thousands of dollars doing this on an organized tour, however. I once did a three-week hike through the Himalayas in Nepal. Along the way I chatted with groups traveling together from Europe and North America. Most of them had spent at least $2,000 on the trip, not counting airfare, and some were still sleeping in tents. I stayed in a different lodge each night—whichever one caught the fancy of the three of us when we arrived in a new village—and ate whatever I wanted off the restaurant menu. In three weeks, I spent about $180. Even if I had hired a personal porter, gorged myself each meal, and drunk beer every night, I doubt I could have spent more than $300.

My wife and I recently hiked the Inca Trail in Peru. It's a spectacular hike through the Andes for four days, ending up at Machu Picchu at sunrise. Demand is high and there are a limited number of spaces available each day, so prices have climbed to nearly $350 each, including a personal porter, the train trip back to Cusco, and entrance to Machu Picchu. If you book this from home, however, with an agency based in the U.S., Canada, or Europe, you will likely pay three or four times this amount. If you have more money than time, that might be worth it. If not, understand that with a little effort, you can usually save a small fortune setting this up with a local provider.

Here are some other examples of trips where alternate transportation is a key part of the adventure. In most cases, these options will allow you to step off the mass tourism treadmill and experience things in a way that is less pre-packaged.

BARGING THE RIVERS OF EUROPE

There are more ways to get around Europe than by bus, train, or plane. You can see a lot of the countryside by boat, getting a whole different view and stopping in towns that are not deluged with tourists. Since many towns and cities were built by waterways originally, you can see a lot with just the boat and your feet or a bike.

There are two ways to do this: on an organized trip that is like a mini-cruise, or by renting a small barge and driving it yourself. On the former, you pay anywhere from $100 per day for a cabin to $50,000 for a group for the whole week—the latter with gourmet meals, top wines, plush staterooms, and private winery visits.

Going it alone is only about $350 to $550 per person per week to rent a six-person barge, but you're the driver and you are on your own for meals. On the plus side, you can stop wherever and whenever you want, spending a night at an inn now and then while you are docked.

BIKING AND SKIING TOURS

A biking tour can be a great way to get away from the crowds and explore the countryside without getting in a car. You see everything at a more leisurely pace and come home in better physical shape than when you left. An organized tour can be anywhere from $400 to $2,500 per week, depending on location, food, and level of accommodation. Experienced bikers who can take care of their own repair problems can do it for less, of course. Many local bike shops can furnish maps, routes, and advice. Some even rent bikes for this purpose. You can do this almost anywhere that traffic or mountains won't kill you.

In Vermont, in the Rockies, or in the Alps, there is a well-developed system of cross-country ski trails that will take you from inn to inn.

SAILING/BOATING

You don't have to be a billionaire mogul to sail from island to island. Just rent a boat and act like a mogul for a week. A self-skippered yacht for a group of six or eight will be $300 to $800 per week per person, depending on the size, location, and season. Hiring a boat with a captain and cook isn't all that much more and saves a lot of hassle. Figure an additional few hundred per person for the week. In some spots, a couple can have a crewed boat all to themselves for this price: the Mediterranean coast of Turkey; the Nile River of Egypt; or the backwaters of Kerala, India (on a converted rice barge) for a start.

Or hook up with a local trip that plies a regular route. You can ride a barge from a Lao border post next to Thailand down to the city of Luang Phrabang, spending one night in a small village along the way. In Indonesia you can get from the island of Flores to the island of Lombok (or vice-versa), stopping at Komodo Island and great snorkeling spots, sleeping on the deck at night.

SCENIC TRAIN TRIPS

Rail travel isn't what it was in its glory days, but there are still plenty of awe-inspiring trips that are an attraction in themselves. Some of them are super-luxurious and expensive, such as the Blue Train through South Africa, the Palace on Wheels in Rajasthan, India, or the many upscale journeys run by Orient-Express. One tier down are ones that are set up for sightseers in developed countries, but are not meant to be five-star. Falling into this category would be the Copper Canyon train in Mexico, the Rocky Mountain Rail Tours trips through the dramatic Canadian Rockies, various trips through the Alps in Europe, the Trans-Siberian Railway, and the select routes in Australia and the U.S. that chug through scenic areas.

Some cheap country train trips are scenic no matter what class you are in. For a few bucks you can get a million-dollar view: the narrow-gauge ride up the Himalayan foothills to Shimla, the journey between Cusco and Puno in Peru, or the Malaysian train leg that goes through the Cameroon Highlands, for instance. If you can take the time to travel in this manner now and then, you will have a whole different sense of movement and geography than those going by plane, rental car, or tour bus.

Ground Transportation Questions for the Contrarian Traveler

1. *Are you going on organized tours because you really like them, or because it was an easy way to purchase a vacation?*

2. *Before you go to a destination, how much time to you spend reading up on local transportation options? Do you know about inexpensive local subways, train systems, and bus systems?*

3. *Do you rent a car because you really need one (because you are renting a villa or moving to a different inn each night, for instance)? Or are you renting a car out of habit?*

4. *Instead of transportation being just a way to get from one place to another, could you make transportation a memorable facet of your trip—by taking an interesting train, bike, or boat trip?*

8

CONTRARIAN SOUVENIR SHOPPING

How Much Would You Pay for That at Home?

*"You'll never meet a traveler who, after five trips, brags,
'Every year I pack heavier.'"*

—Rick Steves, *Europe Through the Back Door*

In the Jeffrey Archer short story "The Steal," Christopher and
Margaret are vacationers on a budget. They have done a lot of
research on the country they are visiting, including what factors to look for when buying a fine handmade Oriental rug.
They are in a carpet shop at the same time as Ray and
Melodie Kendall-Hume, a wealthy, ostentatious, and obnoxious couple. While Christopher and Margaret are friendly
with the proprietor, listening carefully to his explanations
about the various kinds of rugs he has in stock, the other
couple refuses offers of coffee and the man is condescending
to the shop owner. The rich couple ignores advice about what
constitutes a quality carpet and the husband insists on something big and bright for their house. They are in a hurry and
want to get the bargaining over with as soon as possible. They
quickly settle on a price and the carpet seller fills out a receipt
they can show customs on the way home.

Christopher and Margaret sip coffee with the owner and end up getting a much nicer carpet than they expected for their budget, settling on something beautiful that they thought was out of their reach. The price is far less than the big gaudy carpet the other couple purchased. With apologies to Mr. Archer for revealing the ending, the two couples meet again at the airport as they are about to go through customs. Ray talks Christopher and Margaret into switching their carpet for his as they go through the line since theirs is far less expensive. He is already over his duty limit and is trying to avoid paying extra charges. The reader finds out, through the customs inspector, that the big carpet the Kendall-Humes couple bought is worth a fraction of the fine carpet Christopher and Margaret bought. The shopkeeper switched the actual value amounts and took the rude customers for a ride. The couple that got the expensive carpet on the cheap sees a reward for their patience and respect.

The reason this rather utopian story has stuck with me for over a decade is that it is a great summary of the whole souvenir buying experience and an illustration of how so many Western tourists shoot themselves in the foot while shopping abroad. In this example it is carpets, but it could just as easily be pottery, paintings, or woodcarvings. While life is not always as fair as it was in this fictional story, the Johnsons are likely to take the time and do their homework. As a result they end up with better quality items at a better price. The Smiths are more likely to try to duplicate the experience of shopping at Costco. They may not be rich or obnoxious, but they are going to be in a hurry and will not be shopping carefully or smartly. As a result, they are going to get ripped off again and again.

First of all, you don't have to buy souvenirs when you go

on vacation. There is no show-and-tell class at the end of the trip where you must pull out the worthless trinkets you didn't really want anyway. You may stop at twenty souvenir stands, but that doesn't mean you have to pick up anything you won't use or love. If there is something you will treasure, by all means get it. Otherwise, just say no. You'll have less to carry when you go home.

ALL SOUVENIRS ARE NOT CREATED EQUAL

Tourist number one: "Why is there so much crap for sale at every stall you see?"

Tourist number two: "Because people buy it."

That my friends, sums it up. Some seasoned travelers call this the S.S.D.S. Syndrome: "same s&#*, different stall." If dumb tourists are going to buy poor-quality junk over and over, why should craftspeople put more time into creating the good stuff? There's no reason to labor for hours doing something by hand if a machine can do it for cheap and buyers will pay for it anyway.

Do you have items in your attic or basement that you bought on vacation, but haven't looked at since? Did you buy cheesy gifts for people at home that you were embarrassed to give them once you got there? Did you buy a piece of clothing somewhere that looked downright silly once you got it home? Did you buy things in your travels that you ended up giving to Goodwill later? If the answer to any of these questions is yes, then you could have put that money to better use. You could have even given it to a local charity where you were traveling and really done some good.

There's nothing wrong with shopping while you travel, but make sure you are buying something you really want. Most of us have plenty of stuff we don't need at home already. There's no reason to make it worse by buying more stuff we don't need and carrying it home. Besides, the extra stuff might cost you twice: baggage weight limits are getting stricter all the time.

When my wife and I traveled around as backpackers on a budget, I will freely admit we went on some major shopping binges now and then. But we didn't buy junk. Anything we bought was going to have to be shipped back home, which would often cost more than what we paid for the items to begin with. So the items had to be worth keeping or worth giving away as gifts. As a result, our home is filled with interesting items we are proud to display. Many of them come with a story. None of them have a "Made in China" sticker on the bottom. (Though if you've actually been to China and bought something there, that's quite O.K.) We bought quality items we liked for a price someone was happy to take. The transaction usually wasn't quick. Sometimes it took an hour. But in the end we all shook hands and smiled.

BARGAINING IS NORMAL—MOST PLACES

In first-world countries, we do a lot of negotiation, but not when it comes to retail purchases. We look at the price, decide if we're willing to accept it or not, and either pass or purchase. In most of the world, this would seem as alien as a video game. Prices are fluid. The rate depends on the time of day, the inventory level, what the other vendors are charging, and whether you look rich or not. If you are in a hurry, you pay more. If you are a pain in the behind, you pay more. If you are related to the shopkeeper, you pay less. If you are a foreigner but you are good friends with the shopkeeper's cousin…it depends. Each place has a dozen other variables to throw in the mix.

There are whole books written about how to bargain properly in this place or that, but the universal principles are rather simple. Know what you are buying in terms of quality and worth; smile and be friendly; be patient; and be willing to walk away.

If you are set on buying a Tibetan carpet, then do a crash course on Tibetan carpets. Figure out what separates a good one from a shoddy one. Figure out which kinds you like. Find out what they cost at home so you'll have a sense of how much you are saving. Then when you get to where Tibetan carpets are sold, look around and get a feel for prices. Often there's a government-run shop with fixed prices that will give you a sense of the high end. When you feel you have a handle on it, don't budget fifteen minutes to go pick up a rug on the way to the airport. Spend some time and do it right, seeing everything the shopkeeper throws out in front of you and narrowing down your choices to the ones you really want. Then negotiate patiently until a deal is done. In the end you'll have something you will love for life and the seller will have gotten a price that ensures some profit. Everybody wins.

Just keep it civil and remember that both parties are human beings. Anyone who travels frequently has probably laughed at someone who paid five or ten times what they should have for something. We all get taken sooner or later. On the other hand, you don't get a gold medal for outwitting someone who makes $3 a day. This doesn't mean you have to be stupid and pay the first price someone asks, but bargaining hard over the equivalent of five cents at home just makes you look like a jerk. If you really like what someone is selling and are not just buying to be buying, somewhere in the middle is a deal that can happily be struck.

If the idea of bargaining in a store makes you break out in hives or a cold sweat, then pay a little extra and find a good fixed-price shop. In most tourism centers, there is an official one run by the government or a craftsmen/craftswomen cooperative. Prices are higher than you would pay on the street, but not unreasonable. In most cases, the quality is good and you won't see routine things cranked out by a factory.

PUT IT IN PERSPECTIVE

I recently took my mom down to Mexico with me and we visited the popular ruins of Chichen Itzá. The paths leading to the main pyramid are lined with vendors selling lots of junk and some good stuff here and there. Although the vendors are downright mellow compared to their counterparts in Egypt, Morocco, or India, after a while the endless pitches started making me cranky. My mom, who is a retired high school art teacher, struck up a conversation with a wood carver who was selling replicas of ancient Mayan masks that he had carved himself. Against my better judgment, she only half-heartedly bargained with the guy and ended up paying a fair chunk of change for one of his masks. She was happy, though. She could recognize good workmanship and this was a fine piece. "I know this took him a good eight to twelve hours to make," she said as she turned it over in her hands, "and he did a really good job. I'm not going to worry whether I paid $10 too much or not."

While I was concentrating on the bargaining game, she was concentrating on the quality. This goes to the key point of buying something while traveling: What's it worth to *you*?

I had the good fortune of traveling through Indonesia when the Asian currency crisis hit in the late 1990s. Good fortune for me, but terrible fortune for the people who lived there. Suddenly their money was worth one-fourth of what it used to be worth in dollar terms. For those of us with foreign currency, it was a bonanza. We could stay in a three-star hotel for $10, eat in any restaurant we wanted, and hire a car and driver for the day for less than a short cross-town taxi ride at home. When it came to bargaining for souvenirs, however, my heart wasn't in it anymore. I had to go through the motions so everyone could save face, but I wasn't about to try to shave an extra ten cents off a purchase that was already incredibly cheap. More than once I paid more than I could have if I had bargained harder, but I got items I'm still thrilled with and the artisans still did O.K.

Heed local customs, but don't forget that the person on the other end of your transaction has a family to feed, a home to maintain, and a desire to better his or her life. Buy worthwhile things that will truly make you happy and settle on a fair price for them. That's easy to remember and you can sleep well at night.

Souvenir Shopping Questions for the Contrarian Traveler

1. *Do you routinely pack an extra bag for bringing back souvenirs, even when you don't even know what's for sale where you are going?*

2. *Do you research what you are thinking of purchasing ahead of time so you will know what specialties from that area are worth, or do you just wing it after you get there?*

3. *Do you budget the proper amount of time to go shopping in regions where bargaining is the norm—or are you trying to shop quickly like you do at home?*

4. *Do you know the local currency well enough to know how much you are bargaining over and what it's worth in home currency?*

5. *Are you shopping at the best places in town to find what you want, or are you just shopping where the tour bus takes you?*

Part Three

A New Mindset
— *for* —
New Possibilities

9

CONTRARIAN PLANNING

Reservations About Reservations

"If you can spend a perfectly useless afternoon in a perfectly useless manner, you have learned how to live."

—Lin Yutang

When I was in Arequipa, Peru, I was enjoying a Cusqueña black beer on the balcony of my hotel, overlooking the Plaza de Armas. The cathedral was starting to light up as night fell. Down below, a tour bus arrived and the passengers disembarked. They looked tired and stiff, for they had spent the whole day on a bus from Lima. They filed into the lobby to check into their rooms, freshened up quickly, then met at the designated time for dinner in the hotel dining room. Most of them went to bed soon after.

Early the next morning my wife and I came back out to the same balcony for breakfast. Once again, a tour bus was parked below and this same group was boarding the bus. They were going to spend the day in Colca Canyon, which is several hours away. We spent the morning white-water rafting nearby, on a trip we had just booked the day before, for $25 each. In the afternoon we took a leisurely walk around the city, went to one small museum, then met our fellow rafters for happy hour and dinner. As we got back to the hotel around 8:00, the tour bus pulled up again. The passengers spilled out again, looking weary again. They had just gotten back from a twelve-hour day of travel. The next morning they had breakfast, spent only one hour at the main attraction in town, then got on the bus bound for Cusco. We still had another day and a half to explore Arequipa. They had barely seen it.

The Smiths spend a lot of time on a bus like that. When they travel anywhere away from home, for one day or two weeks, everything needs to be worked out ahead of time. Every hotel room is reserved, every activity is planned, and all transportation, apart from taxis, is set up in advance. Either a guidebook or a pre-arranged human guide will always be on hand. At 2:00 P.M. on Thursday, the Smiths know where they will be and what they will be doing. Nothing is left to chance.

When the Johnsons leave home and work behind, they don't trade one routine for another. They don't purchase adventure in advance from a menu of choices: they let adventure happen naturally. Sometimes they book hotels in advance, but sometimes they find places as they go along. They check out the local situation before deciding how to get from one place to another. They leave plenty of time in their schedule for wandering around the city or countryside and they have no qualms about whiling away the afternoon in a town square café or a local swimming hole they stumble upon. Restaurants, sightseeing, and nightlife are experienced with a sense of exploration rather than with a pre-planned checklist. If they need a guide, they hire one locally. If they want quiet and solitude instead, they've got it.

When is the last time you heard an enrapturing travel story from someone who always goes on package tours and has their whole day planned out? Probably never, because nothing surprising is going to happen on those trips unless the bus breaks down. Everyone dutifully files off the bus, takes their photos, surveys the souvenir selection, and gets back on the bus. As a vintage 1963 *Fielding's Guide to Europe* says, "As a member of an escorted tour, you don't even have to know that the Matterhorn isn't a tuba."

Contact with anyone who actually lives nearby is controlled and limited. Opportunities to see what's over the next hill are rare. Nobody is meant to experience anything that is not listed on the brochure. Tourists on these trips spend more, experience less, and often return home exhausted on top of it all.

THE LUXURY OF TIME

Watch American television for a week and you'll get the sense that anything in life can be turned into a contest. Even the simplest activity is only worthwhile if it can be measured, fought over, and discussed in terms of winners and losers. In our society, even when we try hard to avoid it, we are under pressure to stand out, to do better, to win every contest. We're wired to try to come out on top whether in our jobs, our sports contests, our classes, or our excursions to the mall or the car dealer. Raised on this competitive spirit, many travelers have trouble letting go. Many tourists and even round-the-world backpackers carry this reality-TV ethos onto the plane with them like an extra piece of baggage. They race around like sprinters with a stopwatch, somehow thinking people back home are going to measure them by how many places they visited and how many things they checked off some master list.

You know what? Nobody cares. Your friends back home aren't impressed that you visited thirty countries in one year instead of eight, or that you saw every single Egyptian temple along the Nile in four days flat. They really don't care that your trip to Europe took you to six cities in one week. Travel is not a contest and there's no prize waiting at the boarding gate. Stop and smell the papayas. You'll spend less and you'll remember more.

Who is going to spend more on their two-week trip: someone who tries to see every single thing worth seeing in a whole country, or the couple who decides to base themselves in three places only? Who will come out better on accommodation expenses: the couple who books twelve hotels in advance, or the couple who books their first night and then figures the rest out as they go? Which one will spend more on transportation, on food, on guides? Setting up everything in advance can provide peace of mind, but it comes with a premium. Being constantly on the move is costly in two ways—in money and in time.

When people spend most of their vacation going from one place to the next, that becomes the defining factor of their vacation. Many of them want to "do it all," as if this will be their only trip away from home for their entire life. As a result, their impressions of a city are limited to monuments and transportation depots. The only locals they meet are ones trying to sell them something. Far too many of their stories revolve around the process of travel: bus rides, train rides, ferry rides, flights, and time spent waiting for all of the above. While the Johnsons are sitting in a café, watching the local scene, the Smiths are on a bus to the next spot on the checklist. While the Johnsons are checking into their spacious $20 room another traveler turned them onto, the Smiths are being handed keys to a room that looks just like the one they slept in the night before.

Plus who says your whole trip has to be about prime attractions and famous cities anyway? When you haven't planned out every single day, you can get off the beaten path and see a whole different side of a state or country. When you have loads of time in a less-touristed area, you can take things as they come. You can join in on a pick-up soccer game. You can stumble upon interesting things that aren't in any guide-book. You can rent bikes to go exploring or just walk around without a map. You can eat at places that wouldn't know how to cook generic tourist food if their life depended on it. You can spend time with people who don't just see you as a walk-ing wallet, and you can take life at their leisurely pace.

Embracing Unpredictability:
A Vagabond Vacation Tip Sheet
by Rolf Potts

For some strange reason, we Americans see engaged travel to far-away lands as a recurring dream or an exotic temptation, but not something that applies to the here and now. Instead—out of our insane duty to fear, fashion, and monthly payments—we quaran-tine our travels to short, highly regimented bursts. In this way, as we throw our wealth at an abstract notion called "lifestyle," travel becomes just another accessory—a smooth-edged, encapsulated experience that we purchase the same way we buy clothing and furniture.

Fortunately, there's no need to treat your vacation as just another product purchase, even if your schedule doesn't allow for more than a week or two of travel a year. Indeed, if you spend all your travel time on pre-arranged guided tours, in international chain hotels, and eating in predictable restaurants with other tourists, you may as well stay at home and conduct your vacation in a well-heated convention center. Why travel if not to open yourself to the unexpected pleasures of your destination?

With only escape in mind, too many vacationers approach their holidays with a grim resolve, determined to make their experiences live up to their expectations. In our travel daydreams, we transport ourselves to places they believe will be prettier, purer, and simpler than what they encounter at home. The all-inclusive resort industry is structured around such daydreams, but what they usually provide is a generic, standardized product—a lukewarm touristic "Big Mac," when we could be eating a steak.

Sometimes, the easiest alternative to packaged beach resorts is yet another product purchase, the "adventure tour." In America especially (where no experience seems worthy of public mention unless it can be measured, competed, or broadcast before a television audience), modern adventure is associated with extreme sports, like ice climbing, street luge, or high-altitude endurance racing. This is all good fun, but any salty vagabonder will tell you that true adventure is not an experience that can be captured on television or sold like a commodity.

Real adventure is not something that can be itemized in glossy brochures or sports magazines. In fact, having an adventure is sometimes just a matter of going out and allowing things to happen in a strange and amazing new environment—not so much a physical challenge as a psychic one. The secret to adventure away from home is not to carefully seek it out, but to travel in such a way that it finds you. To do this, you first need to overcome the protective habits of home and open yourself up to unpredictability. More often than not, you'll discover that "adventure" is a decision after the fact, a way of deciphering an event or an experience that you can't quite explain.

Remember, the most intriguing experiences and eye-opening encounters come from people whose lifestyles and backgrounds are completely different from your own; these people simply aren't accessible if you confine yourself to luxury chain hotels and tightly-programmed bus tours.

Want to have a memorable vacation, rather than one just as predictable as your workday life? Follow the lessons of the vagabond traveler: pack light, learn to hotel hunt, go public with your transportation, and strike out on foot.

Rolf Potts is the author of Vagabonding: An Uncommon Guide to the Art of Long-Term World Travel. *His travel articles have appeared in* National Geographic Adventure, Condé Nast Traveler, *Salon.com, Slate.com,* Best American Travel Writing 2006, The Best Travel Writing 2006, *and on National Public Radio. His regular musings can be found at Vagablogging.net.*

The Advantage of Local Knowledge

When you make spending decisions based on local prices rather than home prices, you usually get a far better deal. Western Europe and Japan are more expensive than the U.S., so it can make sense to book a rental car or hotel for those places in advance, to take advantage of negotiated rates. In most of the world, with most expenses, you'll do better upon arrival.

One article in *Budget Travel* pointed out that prices for hiring a climbing guide to Gros Piton in St. Lucia start at $100 if booked in advance. If you hire a guide on the spot, it's around $30. This ratio is rather typical around the world, whether you are hiking up a volcano in Java, exploring temples in Nepal, or taking a walking tour of Florence. Every middleman is going to get a cut, so dealing directly with a local cuts out the brokers' margin. Even better, you can negotiate the terms up front, to eliminate shopping stops, for instance, or to determine how much or how little area you want to cover.

When you arrive in a new place for the first time, you probably feel clueless. You don't know your way around, you don't have a feel for prices, you're not sure how much to tip or bargain. After a week, you've got it all down. An amazing thing happens when you start asking other travelers questions, however. You can cut that week down to a couple of days and have more recommendations than you could ever use for restaurants, bars, offbeat things to do, and ways to help your budget. People who have "been there, done that" are usually glad to share what they know. You don't have to be constantly starting from scratch. Some of the most endearing little guesthouses I've stayed in weren't listed in any guidebook. Some of the best restaurants I've been to have never been written up in any magazine article. I've shaved $10 off the price of a taxi ride by just asking someone who has been there a while what it's supposed to cost.

Yes, you can duplicate some of this advice in a virtual way, by frequenting online message boards run by Lonely Planet, Fodor's, and others. So if you do want to book all of your hotel rooms in advance or get a sense of the best area of town to stay, this is time well spent. But things change, advice gets dated, and hotels change owners. Plenty of small hotels still don't have a web site or someone who can answer e-mail in

English. If you get advice at ground level upon arrival, it's always going to be fresh and the options will be greater.

Don't forget that quite a few cities sell savings cards locally that can shave a lot off your sightseeing costs. A $40 Amsterdam Card, for instance, gets you into almost any museum in the city and is good for a canal boat tour and unlimited public transportation. The Carte Musées et Monuments card in Paris is a similar deal, with the $43 three-day card providing access to every worthwhile art museum. You can even go back again to the same museum if you want. It's hard to go wrong with the San Francisco Citypass, which is good for a week of public transportation on top of admission to attractions. With some others, you need to do the math and make sure they're worthwhile. In some cases you would have to run around like crazy all day to make them pay off.

EXCURSIONS AT THE SOURCE

Would you like to sail down the Nile, go trekking in the Himalayas, or white-water rafting in the Andes Mountains? Or camel riding through the desert, island hopping in the tropics?

"Yes," you sigh, "but I can't afford it."

If you're looking at the prices in a glossy adventure travel brochure, you're probably right. But if you follow in the footsteps of long-term travelers and book locally, all of these adventures are easily within your grasp. As in the hiking guide example earlier, the difference is in where your money is going. If you book an adventure trip through an agency in the U.S. or Canada, you're paying a lot of people: the agency owners, the employees who will accompany you (and their expenses), and the local tour company at your destination who supplies guides and equipment. The local portion of that may be quite small in a developing country, but that cost will be marked up substantially to cover the agency's first-world expenses at home, including marketing. So for a typical tour of ten to twenty days, many adventure travelers end up paying $3,000 to $4,000 per person, not including airfare. By the time a couple pays airfare, incidentals, and departure taxes, they could be looking at a $10,000 trip. If they're flying somewhere especially far or difficult to get to, such as New Zealand or South Africa, it can be even more.

Smart travelers simply show up, book their trip, and go when the next group departs. This way they deal with their providers first-hand and all the money goes into their adventure, not into marketing expenses and commissions.

When I was in Nepal, I ended up joining a two-day white-water rafting trip out of Kathmandu. I asked around to find out who was the best operator in town, with the best guides and the best equipment. After I got a definitive answer, I booked my trip with them, traveling down the steepest, fastest river open to the public. My price was $40 per day, including meals, transportation, and one night's lodging in a riverside guesthouse with a bar. Sloshing right beside me in the boat were many people who had booked everything from home, with this side trip part of a $200 per day adventure package.

I've seen this same scene play out around the world, whether it was boating around Krabi in Thailand, taking a weeklong tour through the hill-tribe areas of Vietnam, or touring the Mayan ruins in Mexico. Occasionally you have to book in advance just to secure a spot: the popular Inca Trail in Peru is a good example. In most cases, however, a day or two is about as far out as you have to plan.

Many of the spending decisions you make when you travel have an economic impact that ripples out like a pebble dropped in a pond. When you stay at a locally-owned guesthouse, hire a local rickshaw driver, or eat at a family restaurant, you're directly contributing to the local economy. The same holds true when you book an adventure tour at the source. Ironically, that guide or company you hire is often earning a bigger paycheck from you than they are from the North American adventure company, who is negotiating for a volume discount. At the same time, you are still getting an excellent deal since you've skipped the middleman.

In addition, local providers don't need large economies of scale. Few tour companies in the U.S. or Canada will do an international trip for less than eight people unless the price tag is proportionately high. There's not enough money in it for them except at the luxury end of the market. At the source, however, most companies can provide a more intimate experience for as few as two people, while still making it financially worthwhile for them.

So does this mean you're automatically a sucker if you book your adventure trip from home? No, because there are certainly good reasons for doing that, too. If your schedule is very tight and you need to get back to work on a certain date, it makes lots of sense to let someone else work out all the details in advance. If you're somewhere like rural China or Uzbekistan, where the language barrier is a real issue, having good guides or translators can be essential. And if you're the type who likes to let others map out the decisions or to travel with a built-in group of companions, an organized tour makes sense. Just understand that you are going to pay more and you are going to give up a lot of decision-making power. If you do want to book it in advance, do it with a company that has a good reputation for responsible tourism and has experience in the region. The best tours are small, culturally sensitive, and involved with the local culture rather than sheltering people from it. The really good ones are so plugged in they can take you places you would have a tough time getting to otherwise. See the resources on the web site for ideas on finding tour companies catering to travelers looking for more than a whirlwind of sights and buses.

Planning and Reservations Questions for the Contrarian Traveler

1. Are you the type that absolutely has to have someone else hold your hand every step of your vacation? Or are you taking pre-planned package tours as just a reflex?

2. Have you ever reserved a hotel room in advance and then regretted it after arrival? Could you have done better if you had only reserved one night there and then looked around for a better place?

3. Are you carrying around a checklist of every place you have to see, either physically or mentally? Are you treating your vacation like a contest or a homework assignment?

4. Do you wonder why other people seem to have such interesting stories about people they met or surprises they discovered while they were traveling? Have you noticed that they travel with less of a fixed schedule?

5. Could you have fixed up the adventure or sightseeing tours you took at the destination instead of in advance? How much money would you have saved?

10

CONTRARIAN LIVING

Blurring the Line Between Travel and Life

"Travel spoils you for regular life."
—Bill Barich, *Traveling Light*

Starting off a travel book chapter with the phrase "my wife" is a sure way to get on the bad side of some snooty travel magazine editors and probably a few reviewers. In their eyes no great travel adventure takes place unless one is out there swashbuckling on his or her own, unhindered by a spouse. But the truth is it's my wife who made me realize we didn't have to choose between work and travel. She convinced me that we didn't have to wait until we were old and gray to take long-term journeys. Back when we were still just dating, making barely enough to enjoy living in New York City, she prodded me into jumping off the career treadmill to travel around the world with her for a year.

After both we and the relationship survived that adventure, we saved up some more money, got married, and took off again. Along the way, we figured out that we could have our cake and eat it too. On the first trip, I got some travel writing assignments that paid for part of our trip and we stopped for a while in Istanbul to teach English. Later we did what thousands of other people do each year: got a long-term job in another country. In our case, it was teaching English for over a year in a suburb of Seoul.

When we set off on our first round-the-world trip, most people we knew couldn't fathom the thought of traveling for a year straight. They certainly didn't believe you could travel around the world without being filthy rich, so the first question was how we could afford it. Of course if I asked any of them to add up what they spent each month on just their apartment and utilities, it was always far more than we were spending each month on our trip. The often unspoken question was, "How could you just take off from work like that?" How could two perfectly sane people quit their jobs and just bum around for a year? After all, you are supposed to work like crazy for forty years or so, raise your kids, then travel when you are retired. Isn't that the way it's done?

After our "once in a lifetime opportunity" (in our friends' and employers' eyes) turned into years out of the country, people just gave up and considered us freaks on the fringe of society. But a funny thing happened. We returned home after trip number three with more money in the bank than most of our friends had. And they had been working their tails off nonstop that whole time, with barely time for a vacation, while we had been out seeing the world and learning more than we ever had in college. We now had a wealth of knowledge about geography, world history, religions, international business, and Middle Eastern politics—without cracking one textbook on any of those subjects.

Now, in the following decade, we have a child, a house with a yard, and two cars in the driveway to maintain. But this doesn't mean it's time to get fat watching TV all the time, spending fifty-one weeks a year working. I still routinely take a good six weeks a year to travel, some of it in the U.S., much of it international. We even bought a little house in Mexico where the family can go together and get away from the rat race. My daughter got her first passport when she was three.

VACATION TIME, WORK HABITS, AND STRESS

When the Smiths go on vacation, the goal is to escape reality. They shelter themselves in a resort or routine city hotel for a week. They do what one does in that particular spot, they take their obligatory photos, then return to the grind until the next escape. It's a cycle that will probably repeat itself until they are retired, at which time they won't know what to do with all the free time.

For the Johnsons, travel is not an escape from reality—it is a core part of *their* reality. It's as fundamental to their life as the car and the retirement account. They have made travel, and the education and renewal that come with it, a priority. It is not an escape from what they are and what they do in their "normal life." It is their normal life. They may not have the biggest house on the block or the latest luxury vehicle, but they are rich in experience. They have what most overworked people cannot afford: real leisure time.

In Europe or Australia, going away for five or six weeks is considered quite normal behavior. In the U.S. or Japan, it's next to blasphemous. Americans on average take just ten days vacation per year. This compares to an average of five weeks in Britain or six weeks in Italy or Germany. Then there's France, where work is something you try to fit in between vacation days and weekends. It is rare to meet an American who has gone on vacation for more than two weeks straight and you certainly don't see them traipsing around Southeast Asia or

South America on their six-week holiday like the Dutch. The average American's stay in Cancun is a mere 5.1 days.

You routinely see two- and three-night getaways advertised now: just enough time to start forgetting work and then you're right back in it. According to a survey conducted by the Families and Work Institute, only 14% of Americans take a vacation of two weeks or more. What's worse, most of those are probably retired: 42% of Americans are still doing some sort of work while on "vacation."

Is there anything wrong with bringing some European life balance attitudes across the ocean?

We could at least find some middle ground. In all fairness, this workaholic culture does accomplish something. Statistics show that Europeans in general are not as wealthy as Americans when it comes to net worth and annual salary. Plus the unemployment level is uncomfortably high in some countries, including France and Germany. The U.S. does seem to have higher productivity and on average, a stronger economy. The average American home has expanded from 1,695 square feet thirty years ago to over 2,300 square feet today.

The question is, who's really better off? The society that buys bigger houses than they need, buys more stuff than they can ever use, and buys big vehicles that cost a fortune to fill up? Or the society that spends more of its money and time on leisure and travel? Japan has one of the highest suicide rates in the world and the U.S. leads the world in the use of anti-depressants, so you tell me.

A study of 1,500 women by the Marshfield Clinic found that the fewer vacations women took, the more likely they were to suffer from insomnia or depression, to be stressed out, and to be dissatisfied in their marriage. What's worse, if you're working too much and are too stressed, your memory deteriorates. A study in the journal *Aging and Mental Health* found that people with the highest reported stress performed 11% to 14% worse on memory tests than those under less stress, regardless of age group. You may find that when you finally get to retirement age, you can't remember what it was you wanted to do!

In the world where economics and psychology meet, there's a principle called "hedonic adaptation." The premise is that a salary increase or financial windfall will produce a temporary boost in spirits. After a while, however, your ability to adapt takes over and you get used to the new situation. You probably raise your spending in some way, buy something extra, or increase your monthly bills. Soon, despite the added wealth, you feel no better off than before. This can continue for decades, as a kind of "hedonic treadmill." Spikes in happiness soon fade. (Fortunately, so do spikes in unhappiness, for most people.)

There is hope though. Most studies show that best cure for this pattern is to spend your spare time doing something that is active, not passive. Exercising your mind and body in different ways, making a point of trying activities that are enriching or challenging.

Savvy entrepreneurs and CEOs know that the groundbreaking ideas rarely hit them while they are in the office or burning the midnight oil at home in front of a computer screen. They need to get away: to walk in the woods, to bike through unknown lands, to stroll in a new city. Our mind needs a jolt on a regular basis. It needs to be challenged. If we are to be more than boring creatures of habit, our assumptions need to be rattled by the unfamiliar. As guidebook publisher and PBS television host Rick Steves says, "Travel is freedom. It's recess, and we need it."

"Job" Can Be Loosely Defined...

Right about now you are probably thinking how this is all noble and good, but impractical. "My boss only gives me two weeks' vacation," you say, "and I can never take all of that at one time." Bunk!

First of all, hardly anyone is that indispensable and the world won't fall apart if you leave for two weeks, no matter what your boss thinks. Second, why stay in that job then? We put up with lousy work schedules because U.S. employees don't know any better and dumb employers don't value refreshed employees, despite overwhelming evidence that overworked people are sloppy and unmotivated. Yes, we're coming off a recession, so there's an instinct to hold onto whatever job you have, but demographics are on our side. Despite all the hand-wringing about outsourcing, Chinese imports, and the loss of manufacturing, the demand for skilled workers is already stiff in some sectors and is getting stiffer every quarter. That big bulge of baby boomers is not getting any younger and they're ready to go play some golf. Furthermore, today's twenty-somethings aren't buying into this whole "one size fits all" work culture. They're expecting more vacation time, more flexible schedules, and a life outside the office. What's more, they're getting it. Let the negotiations begin!

That's assuming you want to stick around and work a regular job. Right this minute there is a webmaster working poolside in Costa Rica. There's an ad copywriter with a laptop in one hand and a cocktail in the other, looking out at waves crashing on a beach in Thailand. There's an English teacher sightseeing around Budapest on one of her days off from the local academy. There's a dive master bringing the group back from today's lessons in the Red Sea. There's a crewman manning a yacht somewhere off the coast of Crete. Foreign guys and gals are leading white-water rafting trips down the rivers of the Alps, Andes, and Himalayas. Ski instructors are working both hemispheres at different times of the year. Expatriate managers are leading divisions of global companies in Shanghai, Bangkok, Singapore, London, and Sydney.

Some 4 million Americans live outside the United States, not counting those in the military. Put them all together and this "expatriate nation" would be a medium-sized state— more populated than Connecticut or Oregon. There's no rule saying that working a job has to mean working in the U.S. Imagine the weekend trips these people are taking!

Working Your Way Around the World
by Susan Griffith

Short of emigrating or marrying a native, working abroad is an excellent way to experience a foreign culture from the inside. The plucky American who spends a few months on a Queensland cattle station will have a different tale to tell about Australia from the one who serves behind the bar in a Sydney pub. Yet both will experience the exhilaration of doing something completely unfamiliar in an alien setting.

Anyone with a taste for adventure and a modicum of nerve has the potential for exploring far-flung corners of the globe on very little money. In an ideal world, it would be possible to register with an international employment agency and wait to be assigned to a glamorous job as an underwater photography model in the Caribbean, history coordinator for a European tour company or ski-tow operator in New Zealand. But jobs abroad, like jobs at home, must be ferreted out.

At the risk of oversimplifying the range of choices, the aspiring working traveler either fixes up a definite job before leaving home or takes a gamble on finding something on the spot. A range of mediating organizations and agencies (charitable or commercial, student or general) exists to assist those who wish to fix up a job before leaving home. Some accept a tiny handful of individuals who satisfy stringent requirements; others accept almost anyone. For example, various organizations arrange English tutoring jobs in the Far East (mostly for university graduates) and placements on Israeli kibbutzim.

It would be wrong, of course, to assume that the love (or shortage) of money is at the root of all decisions to work abroad. Many world travelers arrange to live for next to nothing while doing something positive for a local community. For example, enterprising working travelers have participated in interesting projects that range from sports coaching in Ghana to caring for orphans at Mother Teresa's charity in Calcutta. For anyone with a green conscience, numerous conservation organizations throughout the world welcome volunteers for short or long periods to plant trees, count endangered birds, and carry out research on coral reefs. Almost without exception, volunteers must be prepared to cover their own expenses for the privilege of helping.

Most itinerant jobseekers will have to depend on the two industries that survive on seasonal labor: tourism and agriculture. The other major fields of temporary overseas employment are English teaching and au pairing. Both of these options have several dedicated web sites that can be great sources for requirements, rates of pay, and open positions. (See the resources section at ContrarianTraveler.com.)

The casual-cum-seasonal job is always easier to secure on-the-spot than in advance. Finding out where harvesting jobs can be found is a matter of asking around and being in the right place at the right time. Advice will be freely given by expats and fellow travelers if sought. If looking for casual work on farms or trying to fix up a passage on a transatlantic yacht, for example, a visit to a village pub frequented by farmers, yachties, or the local expatriate community is usually worth dozens of speculative applications from home.

Less-structured possibilities abound. Enterprising travelers have managed to earn money by doing a bizarre range of odd jobs, from selling homemade peanut butter, busking on the bagpipes, doing tarot readings on a Mediterranean ferry, or becoming film extras in Cairo or Bombay. None of these options will make you rich, but they can be a nice alternative to cubicle life at home.

Susan Griffith is Work Abroad Editor for Transitions Abroad *and has written many books for working travelers, including* Work Your Way Around the World, Teaching English Abroad, Taking a Gap Year, Gap Years for Grown-ups, *and* The Au Pair & Nanny's Guide to Working Abroad. *These titles are distributed in North America by the Globe Pequot Press (www.globepequot.com).*

All this discussion of how and where to work leaves aside one option—the sabbatical. Some companies are starting to figure out what many travelers have learned on their own: sabbaticals make for better employees. If someone leaves their job for three, six, or twelve months, they return to work far more productive and creative. Instead of being burned out and bored, they are energized and full of ideas. If your employer doesn't offer this option, create your own. If you follow the strategies in this book, you can go away for an extended period and spend far less than you would on day-to-day expenses at home. Once you are out there having time to think and feel, you may realize you want to make some career adjustments anyway. Or you may decide the old definition of a career doesn't make so much sense. Or you may realize you're tired of working so hard for someone else.

If there's something you've always wanted to try as a vocation, take a sabbatical and try it out. Go work in a winery. Go to cooking school. Get your pilot's license. Train to be a ski instructor or a dive master. Become an apprentice under someone who has your dream job. There's even an industry term for this: the "vocation vacation."

DO YOU HAVE TO LIVE WHERE YOU DO NOW...FOREVER?

Some 350,000 Americans live in Mexico. An estimated half million British citizens live in Spain. Some 20,000 American retirees live in Costa Rica. As Bruce Northam says in the book *Globetrotter Dogma*, "Remember, home is where the payments are." There's no rule carved in stone somewhere saying you have to spend your whole life in the same country where you were born. If you were fortunate enough to be born in a land of the free, take advantage of your mobility. Globalization has a down side, but it also has its perks.

If you're hitting social security collection age, you can follow the geriatric trail to God's waiting rooms of Florida and Arizona, or you can go a different route and be better off and more stimulated. Some countries will practically pay you to come live there. If you can document a minimum monthly pension or income of $500, you can retire in Panama at any age and enjoy their *pensionada* program. It includes import duty exemption, half-price entertainment, half-price real estate closings, and hefty discounts on a wide range of costs, from transportation to medical consultations. The economy is stable and the U.S. dollar is the official currency.

Nicaragua is following a similar path. Anyone forty-five years of age or older, with a guaranteed monthly income of at least $400, pays no income tax on out-of-country earnings and household goods (including a car) can be imported duty-free. Supplies brought in to start up a business can also qualify.

These incentive programs aren't limited to Latin America, however. On the European island of Malta, there are no property taxes. Malaysia's "My Second Home" program provides plenty of reasons to move there for retirement. In Malaysia, married couples with one partner aged fifty or older who meet asset or income requirements get an unlimited five-year visa initially and then permanent residency after that. Out-of-country income is tax-exempt, as are imported household goods and a car. Foreign residents can purchase one or two properties and are eligible for a mortgage for 60% of value.

A growing number of countries don't tax income from capital gains, so if you sell a vacation or retirement home at a profit, you could keep it all. There is fine print to pore over, but this currently applies to the rising markets of Argentina, Croatia, Poland, Portugal, and Thailand. The entry point is far lower on top of it all. At a time when beach shacks and lake lots in the U.S. are going for a half million dollars, some of the prices overseas are unbelievable. Delve into international real estate listings and you'll find two-bedroom condos in Ecuador for less than $30,000, Hungarian country castles for under $100,000, beachfront or lakefront lots in Central America for under $20,000, historic colonial homes in Mexico for $80,000, or beachfront condos in Southeast Asia for under $70,000. You'll pay more to be in a gated community with group facilities, but even those properties will usually be half or less what they would cost at home, in dozens of different countries.

Once you move to a country with a lower price of living, of course, your costs drop dramatically. Dan Prescher and Susan Haskins, who run the Mexico office of *International Living*, estimate that a couple could live comfortably in a popular expatriate area of Mexico for under $14,000 per year, including medical care, a part-time maid, and a regular gardener. Figure on roughly $2,000 a month in Granada (Nicaragua), Cuenca (Ecuador), Buenos Aires (Argentina) or Panama City. What would you pay per year to live in a home in the prime cities or beachfronts of the U.S. or Western Europe, at today's prices?

Two things affect how well off you feel: what you make and what you spend. If you can live the good life spending a fraction of what you do now, that's a nice equation. It has to be about quality of life, though, not just the savings. See "Seven Things to Know Before You Invest in Your New Home Overseas."

Seven Things To Know Before You Invest In Your New Home Overseas
by Laura Sheridan

In twenty-five years *International Living* has accumulated some hard-won wisdom, which we'd like to share. Please...leverage our investment of time and money.

1. **Buy title insurance.** Title insurance ensures that a) your new property will indeed belong to you, and b) you are protected against future claims on the property. It generally costs 0.5% of the purchase price or a minimum fee. You can purchase title insurance after a property is in your name, but it's best to contact a title insurance company before you buy your home or land.

2. **Beware of "Margarita Madness."** Don't buy the first house the agent takes you to see. Don't buy on your first visit to a new country. The sea may be sparkling, the palms may be swaying, and the tequila may be flowing, but that's no reason to leave your brains at the border. When buying real estate overseas, invest in more due diligence than you would back home—not less.

3. **Rent first if you're buying as a resident** (this doesn't apply if you're buying solely for investment). Don't buy a home in a new locale until you've spent at least six months living there. Investing in real estate in a place you've only visited or passed through is risky. Selling and re-buying is costly in some parts of the world.

4. **Use an independent attorney, not the developer's attorney.** It is best to find one through the recommendation of another local expat you trust (or, in places where we have them, our International Living Local Office).

5. **Don't expect a multiple listing service (MLS): there won't be one.** To understand what's available for sale in the area where you're interested, you'll have to meet with every real estate agent operating there. They'll all have different listings, some proprietary. Some properties may be listed with more than one agent, but at a different price in each

case. No real estate market in the world is as efficient as that in the U.S. And, a real estate agent who doesn't have an office, his own transportation, and business cards isn't a real estate agent. Don't work with him.

6. **Don't believe any emerging market real estate agent who stands you on a stretch of sand and points out where the marina, the clubhouse, the pool, the dock, or the hotel "will be."** Buy what you see. If all you see is sand, you're investing in sand. If, someday, that sand is improved with roads, electricity, and maybe a day spa—great. But don't pay for the possibility.

7. **Don't move overseas in search of comfort or convenience.** If those are your priorities, stay put. Living overseas is not just about cheap real estate and a low cost of living. If you don't like traveling in a country, aren't charmed by the frustrations of the local way of life, don't appreciate the culture—or the food—then you shouldn't make the move. Cheap real estate doesn't a happy life make in the long run.

Laura Sheridan is the managing editor of International Living, *a publication that has spent over twenty-five years helping readers discover places that are "undervalued...under-appreciated...under-developed...that the masses have yet to find." The company has offices in nine countries.*

BECOMING UNATTACHED

You don't have to buy something overseas to live overseas of course. We Americans tend to look down on renting as something you do when you are young or poor. If you can rent a grand apartment in Buenos Aires or Oaxaca for $400 a month, though, why not just try it out for a while and see if you like it there? For the price of a few nights in a hotel, you have a place of your own for less than you would spend at home. Right now there are hundreds of retired couples bopping around the cities and beaches of the world, staying somewhere for a season or a year, then moving on when they get the urge. No attachments, no closing costs, no accounts to settle. Meanwhile, their investments back home are still compounding.

Many people who have either retired or jumped off the grounded job treadmill do long-term home exchanges. They work out an arrangement to stay in someone's house in say, Paris or Vancouver, while the residents of that house come stay in theirs. It's a simple barter exchange, with no money changing hands. It's a leap of faith, yes, but home exchange organizations have been around for decades and anyone who does it regularly will tell you that problems are very rare.

GET AWAY WHILE YOU CAN

For young people with no attachments, it's almost criminal not to take advantage of the travel opportunities out there. In some cases, you don't even give up anything in terms of life's normal schedule. You can study for a semester or year abroad and not miss a beat for credit hours. Meanwhile, you've added a much more enriching element to your college studies than the same old scene at your local campus. You can do an internship abroad (or at least in a faraway U.S. city) instead of trying something close to home or college. You can take a college summer and work abroad somewhere instead of minding the cash register at The Gap.

It takes a little effort to ferret all this out, but you don't have to be a pioneer really. Plenty of others have already blazed the trail. A magazine I write for regularly, *Transitions*

Abroad, has been around over twenty-five years, pointing the way with nonstop articles and resource listings. Dozens of great web sites are packed with useful links. It just requires a bit of initiative, time, and sense of adventure.

Travel and Life Questions for the Contrarian Traveler

1. *Are you perfectly content with the amount of time you are able to get away? If not, would a job adjustment or more negotiated time off change things for the better?*

2. *If you've always thought it would be nice to invest in a house abroad, what's stopping you from at least starting the research?*

3. *Is there a reason why you live where you do twelve months a year? Can you telecommute from somewhere else part of the time or take a sabbatical? Could you use your skills to work somewhere else?*

4. *If you are a student, have you looked into studying abroad or interning somewhere that will allow you to experience a new place?*

5. *If you are ready to retire, have you thought about all the places in the world where you could spend your time, and thought about how little it would actually cost compared to say, Florida?*

EPILOGUE

The Value of Independent Thought: When the Rules Don't Apply

*"When people are free to do as they please,
they often imitate each other."*

—Eric Hoffer

"Good morning sir!" says a booming voice outside my door. "Time to get up!" I rub my eyes, pull aside the mosquito net, and put on some clothes. Out on my deck I find a loaded coffee press, hot water, and sweet biscuits on a tray. I sit down in one of the comfy armchairs and survey the scene in front of me. The sun is starting to light up the African sky. A few hippos are swimming around in the river, impala are grazing in the tall grass on the other side. In the distant trees, the calls of a dozen different birds compete with a few noisy baboons. After an eagle swoops by and my coffee is finished, I wash up in my lovely bungalow, one of only fifteen bungalows located at this camp. I head down a stone path to breakfast in the open-air restaurant. After some fruit and exquisite pastries, six of us head out on a game drive and see lions, hyenas, wildebeests, warthogs, elephants, and kudu.

A big brunch follows, then some lazing around the swimming pool, high tea, then another game drive with more animal sightings. Out in the bush, there's a sundowner cocktail hour at the end of the day, with the sky turning red and orange. A gourmet dinner follows, accompanied by fine wine from South Africa. After dinner we sip cordials around a roaring fire, hearing the sounds of nothing but animals in the distance. Upon retiring, I find my bed turned down and a local folk tale on my pillow. I sleep soundly on a comfortable mattress, the insects held at bay by screens and netting mounted to hooks on a rail.

This is a typical day experienced by a guest of Orient-Express Safaris in Botswana. It's nowhere close to cheap. In fact, you could buy a late model used car for what it will cost to fly to Africa and spend a week at their three camps in the Okavango Delta. But what an experience!

A trip like this one is not a case where spending a lot of money puts you in a hotel that's just like one at home, or where you are paying extra to be sheltered from the outside world. In this case, you are instead paying a premium to be intimately involved with the outside world. You are on a private concession, with no other camps or vehicles around. You have the wild world to yourself, but without the risks, discomfort, and bad food that often accompany a budget safari. Value traveler that you may be, if you can swing the price this is definitely worth the premium.

This book contains lots of advice on how to shave money off your trip by making shrewd decisions. It shows you how to avoid paying list price by altering one variable or another. Being an independent thinker does not mean trading one set of rules for another, however. Sometimes you just have to say, "Screw all that" and pay the asking price.

There's a time to be frugal and a time to forget what things cost. If you are looking for a special experience, sometimes it requires a special price. There's nothing worse than a shoe-string traveler who is so obsessed about money he skips the experiences that really make a destination magical. In local terms, the price of admission to Machu Picchu in Peru, Petra in Jordan, or Topkapi Palace in Istanbul may seem outrageous. A hot-air balloon ride or a white-water rafting excursion may break the budget for a week. Too bad. Just pay up and have a good time. You don't spend hundreds of dollars to fly somewhere and then balk at the last $50. In the same way, you don't spend months planning a wedding and then have a cheapo honeymoon in a lousy hotel. You don't celebrate your mother's eightieth birthday by taking a chance with an unknown restaurant. You don't sate your child's dreams of going to Disney World by hitting the rides at the county fair. You don't deny your spouse's twentieth wedding anniversary dreams of going to Paris in summer because you're going to have to fly there during high season. Save up your money and go!

Here are a few times when you have to forget what you've learned in this book and just go with the flow.

1. When price is way down on the priority scale. As in the examples above, when it's a special event or occasion, the cost is not the issue. The time, place, and company are far more important than the savings derived by changing something around.

2. When the timing is key. If you are attending something that only happens at a certain time of the year, such as a famous festival, you will have to pay inflated rates—period. Have a good time anyway.

3. When high season is the only good season. There are sometimes very good reasons why people all rush somewhere at the same time: the other times are lousy. When this is the case, you have to pay to play.

4. When package deals or tours are the best deal. In some countries, especially China, Cuba, North Korea, and Vietnam, arranging a trip on your own is expensive and frustrating. When this is the case, suck it up and join the herd.

QUESTION PREVAILING WISDOM

Any how-to guide must make assumptions and generalizations and by nature will have a limited view as to how conditions can change in the future. I challenge you to use the techniques provided in this book to evaluate when the advice is relative and when it is not. A lot can and will change between when this was written and when you plan your next trip. One of the legacy airlines may figure out that the best way to beat Southwest and JetBlue is to offer more services and legroom, not less. One of the cookie-cutter chain hotels may discover that transparent pricing and public spaces that encourage interaction are better ways to draw young guests than simply buying hipper furniture. Perhaps everyone will suddenly rush to Argentina or Laos and they won't be bargains anymore. Maybe everyone will quit going to the Caribbean and huge sales will ensue. Priceline and Hotwire could go out of business or something better could replace them. Nobody knows. You have to pay attention and evaluate your options.

The one thing that will remain constant is your need to ignore the prevailing wisdom that, "This is just the way it is done." Think for yourself. See where the sheep are heading, and how they are getting there, then go the other direction. This takes a tad more effort, yes, but you will be amply rewarded, year after year. Now get out of town!

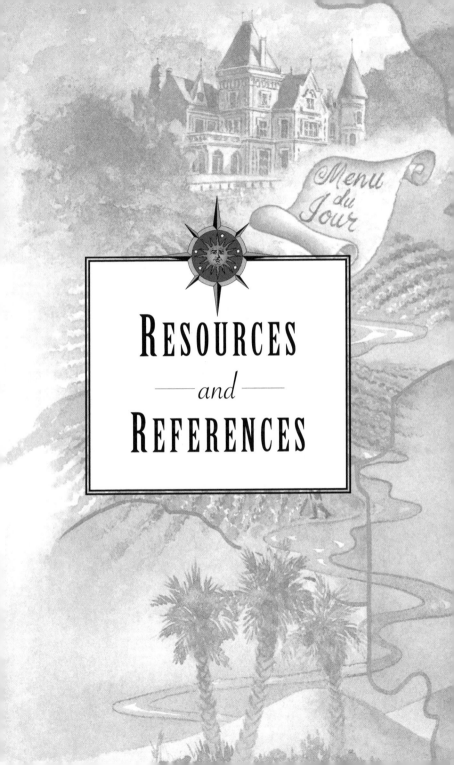

RESOURCES
—and—
REFERENCES

All of the following resources, plus many more, are listed on the accompanying web site: www.ContrarianTraveler.com. There you can click on links and go directly without typing anything else in your browser.

The following are the key resources only, the ones that are leaders in their particular area and still likely to be around a few years after this book is written. All web site names should be preceded by "www." and followed by ".com."

Books

A good guidebook is essential, even when making decisions on the fly, and will easily pay for itself several times over. For independent travelers, the best are usually the ones from Lonely Planet, Rough Guides, Moon Guides, and Footprint Guides. Avid museum-goers and map lovers like the DK Eyewitness guides. Try to compare the options when possible and take the one you like the best. They each have different strengths and are stronger in particular geographic areas.

The Travelers' Tales anthologies make for great reading before departure, while traveling, or after you return home. They give a great flavor of the destination through travel narratives from a variety of writers.

Some of the guest contributors in here have books out that are good for planning independent travel. These include *Vagabonding* by Rolf Potts, *Traveler's Tool Kit* by Rob Sangster, and various working abroad books from Susan Griffith and Clay Hubbs. Richard Sterling's food books contain tales of non-tourist tasting around the world. Check into Ed Perkins' book if you run your own company: *Business Travel When It's Your Money*. For strategies on building and profiting from loyalty, see Joel Widzer's book, *The Penny Pincher's Passport to Luxury Travel*.

Magazines & Newspapers

If you are going to avoid the herds, you need to avoid the
upscale travel magazines that are for people who are not price
sensitive. If you want to read a large circulation title, make it
National Geographic Traveler. Their issues aren't all stuffed
with perfume and purse advertisements and they are more
about travel than pure pampering. The best bet, overall, is
Arthur Frommer's Budget Travel. Arthur doesn't run it anymore,
but the magazine does a fantastic job of showing people on a
modest income how to travel well without spending their life
savings. Each issue is filled with a wealth of great tips. *Outpost*
out of Canada and *Wanderlust* out of England are great reads
imbued with the joy of travel. *Transitions Abroad* magazine's
main focus is on living, working, or studying abroad, but they
also run a lot of useful general travel articles every issue
(including this author's).

Most American newspapers are seeing declining travel
sections as more advertising moves to the internet. It is getting harder for them to maintain high standards and use
material that is not just regurgitated wire service copy.
Newspapers in the five largest cities still maintain sizable
Sunday travel sections, but it is hit and miss in the others.
Some of the best travel information is now in the weekend
editions of the national papers: *USA Today* on Friday and the
Wall Street Journal on Friday and Saturday. Every library has
both, so it's easy to catch up, plus most of *USA Today's* travel
stories are also available free on the web. In other English-
speaking countries, the situation is not so dire yet, so you
can still find useful travel information in large city newspapers outside the U.S.

Web Sites for Information

There are thousands of web sites devoted to travel, but here are the key ones that should positively be bookmarked on your computer.

The guidebook sites LonelyPlanet, RoughGuides, Fodors, and Moon offer up a wealth of reliable and well-researched material for free. In most cases it's a taste rather than a meal, but great for a quick overview and itinerary planning. LonelyPlanet and Fodors also have very active message boards with a lot of members. These are great places to get questions answered or to see what the real situation on the ground is like somewhere. BootsnAll also has an active message board comprised of budget travelers on the move and contains some useful articles and blogs.

To see what other people are saying about a hotel or area, go to TripAdvisor, VirtualTourist, or IgoUgo. These sites specialize in customer-written content and reviews. Be advised that these systems are easy to game, however, and there have been reports of trumped-up reviews written by insiders. It's best to act like an Olympic judging panel: throw out the high and the low scores and average out the rest.

To find out which budget airlines cover specific routes to and within Europe, see WhichBudget.

For links to further information, JohnnyJet is the most comprehensive. This site will lead you to almost anything travel-related you need. Others to turn to for independent travel information include SmarterTravel, GoNomad, TransitionsAbroad, and WorldsCheapestDestinations. Go to Planeta.com for information on responsible tourism.

Web Sites for Booking

Again, there is a seemingly endless supply of sites wanting to book your travel for you. You always need to shop around, but here are some of the most reliable sources for deals.

Two "meta search" sites are good at scanning most of the others to find the best airfare deal: Kayak and Mobissimo. They pull from airline sites and other booking engines. Be advised that there are holes, however, most notably Southwest and many foreign airlines. Sidestep is a similar service that also scans sites for hotel deals.

For finding hotel deals in the U.S., it's hard to beat the prices at Hotwire and Priceline if you go in armed with good information. Before bidding or buying, see the message boards at BiddingForTravel and BetterBidding to see what others have paid for the same city and hotel class. Both can also produce significant savings on rental cars. For comparing rental car prices among the various providers, go to BNM.

There are a variety of sites offering last-minute vacation deals. Inventory varies from week to week, so shop around. These include Site59, 11thHourVacations, LastMinuteTravel, and Hotwire.

E-Mail Subscriptions

You should always subscribe to the e-mail newsletters from your preferred airlines. These can deliver last-minute deals, price drops, and mileage specials. In addition, Travelocity will send fare alerts based on routes and parameters that you choose. When a flight drops below a price you set, you find out immediately.

Other services deliver breaking deals on flights, hotels, and vacation packages to your e-mail address each week. The best are produced by TravelZoo, ShermansTravel, BudgetTravel, and SmarterTravel. The last one will even customize flight deals by your home airport. TripAdvisor will send a weekly e-mail for a specific part of the world you choose—useful if you are planning a trip to a certain spot in the future.

ACKNOWLEDGMENTS

Thanks to Julie Mayo and Jen Leo for getting this project going and to Larry and Susan at Travelers' Tales for seeing it through.

Thanks to all the people who bought *The World's Cheapest Destinations* and made this second book possible, and to the visitors and authors who have made PerceptiveTravel.com a success. Special gratitude goes out to the fellow writers who contributed the additional sections to this book.

Gracias to my family, two people who put up with lots of closed office door time to make this happen.

ABOUT THE AUTHOR

Tim Leffel has dispatched travel articles from five continents and continues to contribute to a wide variety of publications, including some that have managed to stay in business even after his articles appeared. He is a regular columnist at *Transitions Abroad* magazine. He is also the editor of the travel narrative site Perceptive Travel, a publication that is home to some of the best wandering authors in the world (www.perceptivetravel.com).

He has also contributed as a collaborator or ghostwriter to several business books and is the co-author of *Hip-Hop, Inc.: Success Strategies of the Rap Moguls.* He has at times been called a proposal writer, hotel reviewer, ESL teacher, sales manager, music biz marketer, ski instructor, and plenty more titles that will someday make a nice business card collage on the wall.

Leffel splits his time between homes in Nashville, Tennessee and a fishing village in the Yucatán state of Mexico.

The author appears often in the media as a travel expert and is available for interviews. To see more and to get contact information, go to www.TimLeffel.com.

Notes

Notes

Notes